THE MAORI YESTERDAY
TODAY AND TOMORROW

A painting by George French Angas of the famous fighting chief Te Rauparaha, and his son Katu (usually known as Tamihana Te Rauparaha). The elder Rauparaha was a thorn in the side of the early settlers at Wellington.

Reed Tourist Library

THE MAORI

YESTERDAY, TODAY
AND TOMORROW

A. W. REED

A. H. & A. W. REED

WELLINGTON SYDNEY LONDON

First published 1974

A.H. & A.W. REED LTD
182 Wakefield Street, Wellington
51 Whiting Street, Artarmon, NSW 2064
11 Southampton Row, London WC1B 5HA
also
29 Dacre Street, Auckland
165 Cashel Street, Christchurch

ISBN 0 589 00849 8
Library of Congress No: 73-91758

Set in Century on IBM Composer by
A.H. & A.W. Reed Ltd, Wellington
Printed and bound by
Kyodo-Shing Loong Pte. Ltd, Singapore

DEDICATION
For Ava Reed
and Joanna and Richard
with love

CONTENTS

LIST OF ILLUSTRATIONS

COLOUR PLATES

PHOTOGRAPHS

7

INTRODUCTION

NEW ZEALAND is a land of two racial cultures, one numerically dominant, the other a minority group, yet important in national and local affairs.

Until its rediscovery by Europeans, New Zealand was occupied by Polynesians to whom the name "Maori" was given during the eighteenth century. Living in isolation from other Polynesian islanders, they had no identifying name for themselves. For want of a better name early explorers called them "Indians", "natives" (a term that was used officially and unofficially for many years until it fell into universal disrepute), and "New Zealanders". The latter was adequate at first, but as the European population increased it became necessary to differentiate between the brown-skinned and the white-skinned inhabitants.

It was not until the middle of the nineteenth century that the word *Maori* entered freely into the vocabulary with its present meaning. It was a good word, mellifluous, robust, and perfectly suited to a new use. It was first adopted by the indigenous people themselves. According to the standard Maori-English dictionary[1], its original meaning was "normal", "usual", or "ordinary". *Rakau maori* thus meant ordinary trees as compared with those of good timber such as the *totara* and *kauri*; *wai maori* was fresh water, whereas *wai tai* was salt water; *kaipuke maori* was a sailing vessel as distinguished from a steamer; *tangata maori* was a human being as opposed to a supernatural being; and finally, *Maori* was a native inhabitant and not a European, who was termed a *Pakeha*. The latter term is one that may at first puzzle visitors to New Zealand. It means one of predominantly European descent and is a useful term to distinguish such people from Maoris.

Tattooed Maori, wearing black and white huia feathers, a sign of high rank. (National Publicity Studios)

For the benefit of new arrivals to New Zealand it may be mentioned that the vowel sounds in the Maori language are open, each vowel being pronounced. Commonly pronounced Mow-ree, to rhyme with "dowry", the proper sound is Mah-or-ee, the first two vowels being elided to give a richness and depth to the word. Reference to Appendix A will provide guidance to the pronunciation of Maori place names, which are a striking feature of the geographical scene.

The Maori language is spoken by the older Maori people and a limited number of Pakehas, but many younger Maoris and those of mixed ancestry have little knowledge of the language and speak only English. Visitors to New Zealand will therefore have few opportunities of hearing Maori spoken except on formal occasions and at entertainments, though in some remote areas, and in places where there is a concentration of the Maori population, it is still in everyday use. It is a beautiful, musical language, preserving the identity of the race in its historical and legendary allusions. In recent years courses in Maori have been encouraged in schools, colleges, and universities, and interest is increasing.

As with language, so with costume. No matter what glamorous publicity they may have seen in tourist literature before arrival, visitors will not see Maoris in traditional dress except at official welcomes and entertainments, where representatives of the Maori community take pride in presenting colourful songs, dances, and oratory. It is part of *maoritanga*—the consciousness of being a Maori, as expressed in various forms, including carving, weaving, traditional history, chants, songs and dances, the lore of the *whare wananga* (the ancient schools of learning), and the dominance of the *marae* (the meeting place of tribe and subtribe).

Miss Maureen Kingi, a former Miss Zealand, in Maori costume at Pohutu Geyser, Whakarewarewa, Rotorua. (National Publicity Studios)

The Maori of today is a New Zealander with full and equal rights of citizenship. His pride in his lineage and culture is shared by his Pakeha friends, and over a period of nearly two hundred years there has been a fusion of the two races by intermarriage. It can be said with confidence that the New Zealand Pakeha respects and admires his Maori compatriots, who have distinguished themselves both in sport and in war. This is not to say that there are not some tensions as younger people come from rural areas to the cities with inadequate education and are forced to find substandard accommodation. Nevertheless Maoris are accepted

Charles Bennett, DSO, MA, former High Commissioner to Malaya, now President NZ Labour Party. (National Publicity Studios)

as equals and as an essential part of the community. Their problems and achievements will be discussed in the final chapters.

One thing is certain: we cannot pretend to know or to understand New Zealand until we accept it as a nation of a single people, of Maori and Pakeha working and playing together with mutual understanding and faith in the future.

References   1. *A Dictionary of the Maori Language,* H.W. Williams. Government Printer.

A famous painting by Sam Stuart of a pa (fortified village) on the Wanganui River, showing palisades, houses, and the marae (open courtyard), which was the centre of activity in the village. (Auckland Art Gallery)

CHAPTER 1

IN THE BEGINNING

From the conception the increase,
From the increase the thought,
From the thought the remembrance,
From the remembrance the consciousness,
From the consciousness the desire . . . .

The world became fruitful;
It dwelt with the feeble glimmering;
It brought forth night:
The great night, the long night . . . .

From the nothing the begetting,
From the nothing the increase,
From the nothing the abundance,
The power of increasing
The living breath.
It dwelt with the empty space,
And produced the atmosphere above . . . .

And the moon sprang forth . . .
And thence proceeded the sun;
They were thrown up above,
As the chief eyes of heaven:
Then the heavens became light,
The early dawn, the early day,
The mid-day.
The blaze of day from the sky.

15

COSMOGONIC MYTHS, departmental gods, legends, genealogies, ancient chants, stories of gods and ancestral heroes,
tales of enchanted objects, spirit manifestations, personi-
fications of natural phenomena—all are necessary to an
understanding of the Maori's Polynesian forbears and their
descendants of the twentieth century.

So we return through the long years of history and
legend to the Kore, the Nothingness that was before Creation, to the endless night and chaos and the first stirrings
of feeling and thought. The Nothingness was succeeded by
the begetting, the living breath—and then the explosion of
light and life. The Maori of long ago not only lived close to
the natural world; he was a part of it. The innermost secrets
of the universe were given to those to whom the gods revealed knowledge. In the beginning there were no gods, no
earth, no sea, no sky. Out of the desire came the two primal
parent gods, **Rangi-nui-e-tu-nei**, the Sky Father, and **Papa-
tu-a-nuku**, the Earth Mother. Locked in an age-long em-
brace, the Earth Mother gave birth to seventy children who
inhabited the dark spaces between their parents. These
were the gods of the Maori pantheon, of whom six were
regarded as departmental gods—**Tane** of the many names,
the god of forests; **Tangaroa**, the god of the sea; **Tu-matauenga**, the god of mankind and, significantly, of warfare;
Rongo, the god of cultivated foods and peace; **Haumia-
tiketike**, the god of fernroot, the unfailing staple diet when
other food was scarce; and **Tawhiri-matea**, the god of the
winds.

Living in darkness, with little room to move, the seventy
male gods longed for light and air. One after another they
strove to separate their parents; one after another they failed
until Tane put forth his strength and hurled the Sky Father
far out into space. Many were the noble deeds of Tane the

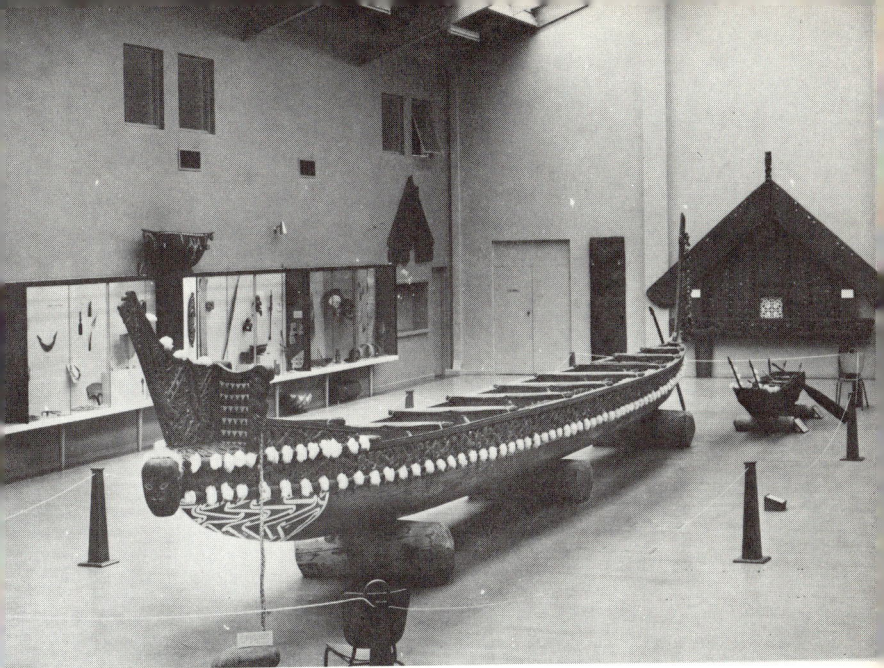

Maori Exhibits Hall at Canterbury Museum, Christchurch. (National Publicity Studios)

forest god, known also as Tane-mahuta the origin of trees, Tane-mataahi, the father of birds, Tane the fertiliser. He adorned Mother Earth with verdure, Father Sky with sun, moon, and stars. The tears of Rangi fell on Papa, the sun shone, the trees and plants of Tane flourished. Earth and Sky were made beautiful. Only Tawhiri the wind god was at enmity with his brothers. He followed his father while they remained with their mother; he fought against the sea god, the forest god, the war god. Tu alone, the god of mankind, was able to withstand him.

That is the Maori story of the beginning of creation. In his search for the female element in nature Tane mated with an endless succession of personifications. Referring to the

significance of the complex scheme of belief in gods, powers
of fertility, and the vital essence on which all things depend,
in *Economics of the New Zealand Maori*[1] Raymond Firth
wrote: "It became fairly clear that these guardian deities
and their *tapu*, and the rich galaxy of supernatural beings
with whom the Maori delighted to people his world of folklore, are not merely the chance creation of a mythopoetic
mind, which loves to think in imagery and to personify
natural phenomena. Their genesis must be explained on
more fundamental grounds. The host of personified elemen-
tal phenomena, the quaint and intricate mythology which
deals with Nature in all her moods and disguises, is the out-
come not of the unfettered mythic fancies of a poetic mind,
but a vital interest in things upon which the Maori depends
for his existence and welfare."

The land, too, was all-important. It was the sustainer of
life. Many are the proverbial sayings in praise of land, such
as: Food supplies the blood of man, his welfare depends on
the land; The treasure of land will persist, human possessions will not.

Dependence on the fruitfulness of land and sea was
doubtless responsible for the institution of *tapu*, to which
Professor Firth refers. The felling of trees, the growing and
gathering of food, the process of cooking, and industry of
every kind were subject to the restrictions of *tapu*—that
almost indefinable element that was associated with the
gods and has its counterpart in Hebrew and Christian religion in the word "holy". It embraced all that was
"separated" from common usage. It was the embodiment
of supernatural power. To defy or neglect *tapu* was to court
death. Usually translated as "sacred", or "forbidden", *tapu*
could be circumvented only by the incantations and spells
of the *tohunga*, the priests who guarded the "baskets of

knowledge" brought by Tane from the over-worlds to mankind.

Before a forest tree could be cut down, Tane had to be propitiated by the recital of incantations. Cooked food was destructive of *tapu* to such an extent that chips of wood cut by the adzes when making a canoe would never be used for oven fires. Women were strictly forbidden to be present at canoe making or house building, but were used to destroy the *tapu* prior to the opening of a meeting house. The head of a chief was especially *tapu*, as also were burial grounds. A *tapu* could be laid on any object or area of land to make it forbidden property. The institution was used in many ways in relation to land, of which the Maori was a notable conservationist.

The schools of learning conducted by the *tohunga* were *tapu*, the pupils being confined to men of chiefly rank. Knowledge, which included genealogies, astronomical lore, agriculture and similar subjects relating to everyday pursuits as well as to esoteric knowledge, had first been brought to earth by Tane. How natural phenomena were regarded as supernatural manifestations may be illustrated by the re-markable exploits of Tane in fathering a variety of trees, plants, and birds, as well as mountain stones and flood waters, on Mumu-hango and other female semi-deities. Further experiments with a second generation of personi-fications produced *taniwha* (monsters), insects, lizards, reefs, rocks, gravel, and sand.

Tane-matua (Tane the Parent, so known because of his generative powers) sought for the elusive female element in vain until he took the advice of his Earth-Mother Papa. "Go to your ancestor Ocean," she advised him. "He is grumbling there in the distance. When you reach the beach at Kura-waka, gather up the earth in human form."

Agricultural instruments used by ancient Maoris, and a kumara god which was invoked to bring good crops. (National Publicity Studios)

Tane was at last successful. He lay upon the image, breathed life into it and so formed the first woman, the crown of creation, Hine-ahu-one, whose womb was the female element denied to the gods. The creation of man by Tu-matauenga was a similar but less spectacular event.

So, in the story of the Maori gods, we have an explanation of every natural phenomenon from the creation of land, sea, and sky to the emergence of life and the immortal element of fertility, without which land and sea would be sterile.

The concept of creation has much significance in Maori

thought. It is a refinement of similar beliefs held by other Polynesian peoples, but differing from them in many respects, and especially regarding the honour accorded Tane, the forest god. Elsewhere in Polynesia Tangaroa, the god of the sea, is regarded as all-powerful, though Tane holds an honoured place. While the Maori was dependent on the sea as well as the land for his food, the latter was naturally more important, whereas in the smaller Pacific islands the sea larder was of more importance than that of the land.

References. 1. *Economics of the New Zealand Maori.* Raymond Firth. Government Printer.

A tangi. An early painting by R.A. Oliver of a group of mourners. The tangi is still an occasion for the release of emotion in an uninhibited display of grief. (Alexander Turnbull Library)

CHAPTER 2

THE PEOPLING OF A NEW LAND

Pipitori nga kanohi; kokotaia nga waewae;
whenua i mamao, tenei rawa.
With the sharp eye of the white-breasted tit, and its quick feet,
a distant land will soon be gained.

TRADITION on the one hand, and archaeological, anthropological and linguistic research on the other, are not, as many believe, contradictory. They are facets of the same essential truth. The fascinating legendary account of the discovery of New Zealand, the arrival of the canoes of the Fleet, and the exploration of the country will be told later. Contradictions will be found in various tribal versions but, similarly, unanimity of opinion amongst scholars and research workers has yet to be achieved. The facts on which they are agreed are that some four thousand years or more ago the Caucasian ancestors of the Maori race left their homes in South-east Asia and on the south coast of China. They embarked on a voyage that led generation after generation through various island groups until they reached their final Pacific "homeland" in Eastern Polynesia. From there this adventurous seafaring people populated the scattered island groups of the Pacific, travelling northwards to Hawaii, eastwards to the Marquesas and far-away Easter Island, westward to Tonga, Samoa and the Cook Islands, and southward to New Zealand.

The almost incredible feat of sailing thousands of miles from Tahiti, or even from the nearer Cook group, in canoes,

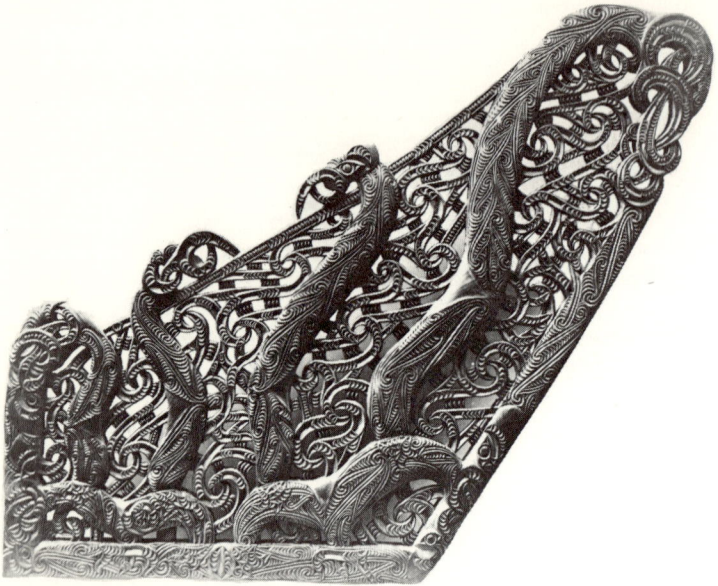

Carved sternpiece of Maori war canoe, Ngapuhi type, used by northern tribes. (National Publicity Studios)

without charts and scientific navigational aids, has provoked animated discussion amongst students and scientists in recent years. One theory, supported by painstaking research, is that the populating of distant islands, and particularly New Zealand, could have been effected only by accidental drift voyages. Once the castaways arrived at a distant island they had no hope of returning to their homeland. Fishing canoes would not be likely to contain women, but others, travelling comparatively short distances from one island to another on friendly visits would no doubt include members of both sexes. Blown off course by unexpected storms they might eventually arrive at the shores of New Zealand and, in a thousand years or more, their descendants could, quite reasonably, have increased to a population of one to two hundred thousand.

Other students maintain that the early Polynesian seafarers had an accurate knowledge of trade winds and ocean currents and were skilled students of astronomy. Dr David Lewis, a firm believer in this theory, recently undertook a long Pacific voyage without compass or charts but with the assistance of an islander who had inherited the skills of his seafaring ancestors, and was successful in making a planned landfall. Maori tradition supports Lewis's theory and embodies several convincing accounts of return voyages to Hawaiki, the homeland at Tahiti.

Under whatever conditions the voyages were made, it is certain that the first visitors arrived at New Zealand some time about or before the year 1000 AD. Archaeological discoveries of recent years, together with carbon-dating techniques, are tending to put the date a good deal earlier.

The pioneers were not the Maori people of today. That they were Polynesians is certain. This we know from the discovery of artifacts such as stone adzes that have the same characteristics as others found in various Polynesian islands. The material culture of the earlier arrivals differed in many respects from that of those who followed them.

Although forest, river, lake, and sea provided adequate food resources, the first-comers must have found it an inhospitable land in comparison with their earlier home with its luscious fruit and tropical warmth. One of the principal sources of food was the *moa*, several species of which were plentiful at that time. These birds ranged from comparatively small species to large birds exceeding the emu and ostrich in size. They were found mainly on tussock land

and in open spaces, and were hunted relentlessly with spear and snare. For some time the first Polynesian settlers became a semi-nomadic people, always moving on to new hunting grounds, seldom penetrating the forest lands. Excavations have revealed a variety of their ornaments and tools, including necklaces, fish hooks and spear-points made from *moa* bones. In time permanent settlements were established, and the people made greater use of the resources of the country by fishing, birdhunting expeditions in the forest, and gathering shellfish. Artifacts that have been recovered include needles, chisels for tattooing, fish hooks of various kinds, amulets, and cloak pins, but a singular lack of weapons, leading to the conclusion that they were a peaceful, industrious, and contented people. To distinguish them from later arrivals they are now known as "Moahunters" or, less frequently, the "Archaic" Maori as distinct from the "Classical" Maori, whose traditions often refer to their predecessors as the *tangata whenua*, the "people of the land".

Some three or four hundred years after the advent of the Moa-hunters a steady migration of their successors began. The population of Ra'iatea and Tahiti had increased to such an extent that there was a severe shortage of food, which resulted in tribal wars. There seems little doubt that a series of carefully planned voyages occurred during this period. Huge double canoes with a connecting platform, surmounted by a roofed structure and equipped with one or two sails and a steering oar, provided seaworthy craft for the long voyage. Sailing instructions appear to have been handed down from earlier arrivals who had succeeded in returning to the tropical homeland. The voyage may well have been broken at intermediate stopping places such as the Cook Islands, which are populated by near relatives of

Hunting the moa, a reconstruction of the giant bird hunted to extinction by the early Maoris. (National Publicity Studios)

the New Zealand Maori, and who also bear the racial appellation Maori. Prepared for the more inclement climate and comparative paucity of food in the new land, supplies of *kumara* (sweet potatoes), yams and *taro*, together with dogs and rats (berry-eating rodents that provided succulent food) were taken aboard the canoes and planted or released on arrival. The *aute* or paper mulberry, intended to provide clothing, was also brought to New Zealand but did not flourish.

The newcomers were strong and virile and had little difficulty in absorbing the Moa-hunting people, either by intermarriage or conquest. Both races were of common Polynesian origin and had many affinities, but the later arrivals were better equipped to cope with the new conditions.

The archaeologist of the present day is steadily reconstructing the picture of settlement of the two principal waves of migration. Unlike the traditional accounts, however, his findings cannot be specific in pinpointing the canoes' dates and landfall localities. Tradition is not to be accepted as fact with the status of recorded, verifiable records, but it does contain the germ of truth, interpreted through vivid word pictures. The Maori can determine chronology through carefully preserved genealogies, certainly to the beginning of the Classic period and possibly earlier still. He looks with pride on the accomplishment of his ancestors, and can claim that his calculations are not far removed from those of the archaeologist.

Faintly through the mists of those far-off days come the spectral shapes of half-men, half-gods who may have been the first of the human race to penetrate the southern seas— among them Hui te Rangiora, who is believed to have sighted icebergs. More clearly there emerges the demigod Maui, famed as a fisher-up of islands throughout Polynesia. His greatest feat was the dragging up of the North Island from the sea bed, complete with the house of Tonganui, the son of the sea god, together with forests and lakes and

Maori artifacts including crayfish and eel traps used in various aspects of fishing in olden times. (National Publicity Studios)

cooking fires. A glance at the map of the North Island will clearly reveal the shape of *Te Ika a Maui*, the Fish of Maui. As early as 1819 the Rev Samuel Marsden recorded the words of a *tohunga* of Hokianga: "I wished to learn from him who was the first man in New Zealand. He answered that the first man who visited New Zealand, from whence all originated, was Mowhee [Maui]; and that he left his own country with his followers on account of public troubles, and was afterwards conducted by the god of thunder to Showrakkee [Hauraki] or what we call the river Thames. He said that Taurekke [Tawhaki], the god of

The huge waka taua *(war canoe) in the Auckland Institute and Museum, Te Toki-a-Tapere, is capable of holding a hundred warriors. The prow is a fine example of delicate tracery in wood with characteristic spirals. (K. & J. Bigwood)*

Maori girls performing the graceful actions of the poi *dance, the* piupiu *or dance skirts and the* taniko *woven bodices are adaptations of a more ancient costume. (K. & J. Bigwood)*

thunder, sat at the head of his canoe and brought him safe to land. His name is held in great veneration."

Even more clearly comes Kupe, his friend Ngahue, and his wife Kearoa, who not only sailed round the coast, landing at various localities, but also conferred place names that have survived to the present day. It was Kearoa who gave the accepted name to the new land. Sighting it from far out at sea, she exclaimed: "He ao! He ao!" (A cloud! A cloud!), and from this derived the full name Aotearoa, usually translated as Land of the Long White Cloud. From Arahura, on the west coast of the South Island, he brought home a lump of greenstone, the hard jadelike nephrite for which New Zealand is famed. A further souvenir of his voyage was a piece of preserved *moa* flesh—and, even more important, directions on how to sail to the newly-discovered land. The date of his visit is placed about the year 950 AD.

Another expedition, believed to have occurred some two hundred years later, was that of Toi, an aged Polynesian who left Hawaiki in search of his grandson Whatonga, whose canoe had been swept out to sea in a sudden storm. Arriving at the Bay of Plenty, Toi gave up the search and settled among the *tangata whenua* who were already in possession of the area. Eventually he was joined by his grandson.

Shortly afterwards the chief Manaia fled from the homeland with his sworn enemy Nuku in hot pursuit. The chase ended at Paekakariki, some forty kilometres north of Wellington, where Manaia called for help on the god of the sea. The gale that dashed Nuku's canoe to pieces formed the tall sand dunes of that stretch of stormy west coast.

It is possible that supplies of *kumara* were imported on occasional unrecorded voyages during the next two hundred years. About the middle of the fourteenth century there

"The Coming of the Maori", a painting by Marcus King. (National Publicity Studios)

occurred the greatest event in Maori history—the arrival of the Fleet. It must be admitted that doubts have been cast on the concept of a *heke*, a large planned migration by a fleet of oceangoing canoes, but it may be conceded that the canoes, whose names are enshrined in legend and song, together with the names of their commanders and in some cases of the crews, probably arrived within the space of a few years.

It is tempting to relate at length the legends that have gathered round these illustrious vessels—*Te Arawa* (The Shark), *Tainui* (Great Tide), *Mataatua* (Face of a God), *Kurahaupo* (Storm Cloud), *Tokomaru* (Staff of the War God), and others[1], but we must hasten to tell what happened to the descendants of the men of the Fleet.

Landings were made on several parts of the North Island coastal settlements were formed, and claims to forest, mountain, river, lake, and fishing grounds were quickly made. The principal tribal boundaries were therefore determined shortly after the Great Migration. Descent from the *waka*, the ancestral canoe, is still the proud boast of many families throughout the country.

References. 1. *How the Maoris Came to New Zealand.* A.W. Reed. Reed Education.

A typical meeting house in an attractive setting at Te Kuiti. The traditional carvings and rafter patterns contrast with the modern cars and costumes. (Fritz Prenzel)

The art of carving has not been lost. Young Maoris are trained in skills of their forbears, but with modern tools, at the Maori Institute at Rotorua. (Fritz Prenzel)

CHAPTER 3

THE CLASSICAL MAORI IN EVOLUTION

Tohea, ki te tohe o te kai.

Be active, persevere in everything, just as you have to
work hard for food.

THE CLIMATE of New Zealand before the twelfth century
may have been warmer than at present, but by the time the
Classical Maori arrived it was growing colder and drier. The
new arrivals discovered that the South Island was a relatively cold, rugged, mountainous land. Little settlement
took place there. Parts of the North Island were pleasant in
spring, summer, and autumn, but the settlers were probably
dismayed by the bleak winter weather, for in the homeland
the gentler climate allowed crops to be harvested all the
year round. Large settlements were formed in the Bay of
Islands, the Tamaki isthmus, the Waikato and Hauraki
plains, the Bay of Plenty and Poverty Bay, Rotorua and
Taranaki, and other areas where the climate and soil were
most favourable.

There were no land animals except birds, no forest fruits
except the small berries of the *hinau* and *tawa* trees in the
inland areas, and the larger *karaka* berries of the coastal
districts. Fortunately there were myriads of birds, far more
than in the tropical islands—plump wood-pigeons, tasty
kiwis and *wekas*, ducks and other birds that could be
caught and killed by means of long spears, snares, nets, and
sometimes even by hand. The lakes and rivers teemed with
freshwater fish, the coastal waters with *moki*, cod, snapper,

Black weka, bird used by Maoris as a food source. (National Publicity Studios)

groper, *tarakihi*, and big-game fish—sharks and swordfish—and, in the far south, seals and muttonbirds.

The New Zealand Maori was forced to prepare the ground for his cultivated food, clearing away bracken and scrub, loosening the earth, removing roots, storing tubers and planting them, bringing sand and gravel and ashes to lighten and enrich the soil, and keeping the *kumara* mounds heaped up.

There was only one plant that provided an unfailing source of vegetable food throughout the year, the bracken fern. The rhizome or root was dug up, but it was stringy and tasteless and required a great deal of preparation before baking into flat cakes on the ashes of a fire.

Bird-hunting was developed to a fine art; huge weirs and baskets were constructed to catch eels and lampreys; nets half a kilometre or more in length were used to catch sea fish, and large canoes were built to take fishermen to the off-shore fishing grounds. This in turn meant that giant trees such as the *kauri* and *totara* had to be felled and shaped, and taken on skids to the shore.

An old Maori sorting a fine crop of kumara for the pit. (Alexander Turnbull Library, Northwood Collection)

It is not difficult to imagine what the onset of winter meant to people who had come from a land where it was always summer. Vast quantities of food had to be preserved and kept for the lean winter months. *Kumara* and fish were dried and stored in pits and storehouses or on elevated platforms to keep them safe from damp, and from rats, dogs, and ground-birds. The Maoris had no vessels for holding liquids until they grew the *hue* (gourd plant) from which calabashes were made; in these, birds were preserved in their own fat.

Substantial houses were built as protection from cold and wet weather. Tools were made for felling trees and shaping them into posts and panels, reeds were gathered for thatching, and *toetoe* and bracken stalks for lining the walls. Fires were lit on winter nights; supplies of firewood were gathered for house and cooking fires. Warmer rainproof clothing was needed. The flax plant provided leaves and fibre for mats and cloaks as well as rope for lashing the timbers of houses and canoes.

Of necessity men and women were forced to work long hours. The arts of Maori carving and weaving were evolved, and in the course of time essential articles for everyday use were embellished with wonderfully decorative and functional designs.

Sites for villages were chosen for reasons of defence and proximity to water and food supplies. The strength of a village depended on the united efforts of all its occupants. Families grew in size and became clans, and often grew into large tribes containing smaller groups, all banding together in time of war. It became necessary to defend plantations and hunting and fishing grounds. The tribes developed a strong affection for the tribal lands and were ready to defend them to the death. Their fortified villages were sur-

Representation of old-time fortified pa *on a strategic headland, by Marcus King. (National Publicity Studios)*

rounded by stockades. War parties went out to seek revenge for insults. As some tribes became larger and stronger, the weaker ones were driven from their homes. Men and women captured in warfare were killed and eaten by the conquerors, or kept as slaves to do the menial work of the village.

Changes in life style occurred, quickly at first in order that the pioneers and their immediate descendants might survive. Even greater changes took place more gradually as the Polynesian settlers developed into the Maori race with its own manners and customs, its own kinds of weapons, buildings, tools, clothes, songs and dances, history and legends, social system, laws, and decorative arts. The original language underwent changes. The legends of their forefathers and their gods began to take on new interpretations.

Tohunga (experts) were trained not only in religion but in carving, house and canoe building, and other important tasks. The transition from Polynesian settler to Classical Maori was a process that lasted several hundred years.

There is still fascination in reconstructing life and customs that slowly evolved over the years and were then changed so suddenly and dramatically when men of the western world arrived in New Zealand—a fascination that is demonstrated by the recent revival of interest in Maori language, traditional arts and crafts, songs and dances, and in serious anthropological research.

The isolation that resulted from the cessation of ocean voyages shortly after the arrival of the Fleet was responsible

A meeting of friends in the 1840s, with Mount Egmont in the distance. Painting by George French Angas. (Alexander Turnbull Library)

for revolutionary changes of habit and ultimately of social organisation and attitudes of mind. The vast extent of country available to a handful of Polynesian settlers and the wide dispersal of their landing places would seem at first to have given each small tribe ample opportunity to select the land it favoured; yet no sooner had the canoes landed than there was a struggle for land between men of the *Arawa* and the *Tainui* canoes. In a short space of time explorers were ranging widely throughout the North Island, laying claim to the best territory. As years passed by and new generations succeeded the pioneers, the population increased, tribal boundaries were enlarged, and conflict inevitably followed.

We cannot tell how long the territorial struggles lasted, but eventually the tribal areas became clearly defined. Jealousy between the descendants of the canoes, and the long years of aggression doubtless fostered the warlike proclivities of the Maori. Strong palisaded villages termed *pa* were built on hilltops and other impregnable positions as a defence against raiders. *Kainga* (unfortified villages) were sited close to the cultivated areas, for the Maori needed to supplement the uncertain harvest of the hunter and fisherman by cultivating the *kumara* plants imported from the homeland. The *pa* remained a place of refuge, but was in constant occupation in case of unexpected attack.

In the course of time the tribes (*iwi*) were subdivided into sub-tribes (*hapu*). The smallest unit in the social organisation was the family (*whanau*)—a much larger group than in European communities. Each *hapu* or *whanau* had its own clearly defined forest land for hunting and, in coastal districts, fishing grounds. The individual might lay claim to his own particular area, but in fact it was possessed by the *whanau* as a group. The principle extended to the *hapu* and the *iwi*. This combination of personal and communal rights

provided an almost insoluble problem when European land
purchases were being negotiated.

The leaders of the tribe were the *ariki*, men or occasionally women, who could trace direct descent from the
principal chiefs who arrived in the Fleet. The principal chief
(*upoko ariki*) was required to show positive gifts of leadership as well as an impeccable genealogy. In time of war he
might depend on the advice of lesser chiefs, but he wielded
ultimate authority. The *ariki* was frequently also a *tohunga*,
but whether or not he had attained supernatural knowledge,
his person, and especially his head, was *tapu*. He was re-

Oil painting depicting life in an old-time Maori pa, *by Marcus King.*
(National Publicity Studios)

Watercolour by George French Angas. A korero *or council of chiefs at Te Wherowhero's marae in 1847. (Alexander Turnbull Library)*

garded as the *taumanu* or resting place of the gods; in times of peace he took a lesser part in community affairs, when men and women of authority did not hesitate to express forthright opinions on the *marae* or in the meeting house about matters affecting the welfare of the tribe. In this connection it may be mentioned that the *marae*, which in other parts of Polynesia was a sacred place corresponding with the temple in European countries, was in New Zealand the communal meeting place, a stage for orators, and a place for social activities of every kind, including games and entertainments. The *marae* was—and still is—the focal point of everything that pertains to the welfare of a Maori community.

Next to the *ariki* came the *rangatira*—men and women

of noble birth who were entitled to state their opinions boldly on the *marae*. They were the freemen and women of the Maori people and have been described as the heredi- tary aristocracy. It is usually stated that the three strata of Maori society were the chiefs (*ariki* and *rangatira*) com- moners (*tutua*), and slaves. The *tutua* class, composed of those who married into younger branches of their families and their offspring, were reluctant to accept this classifi- cation. There is much to be said for the opinion that every freeman or woman except those who were deliberately downgraded, was a *rangatira*. The lowest class was that of the slaves, usually captives taken in battle. No matter how elevated in rank they might have been before capture, their *mana* was lost, and they were reduced to a position of ser- vitude, subject to every whim of the *rangatira*, even to the point of being killed and eaten. Their children were also slaves, but the offspring of a slave wife and *rangatira* hus- band was born free.

The *tohunga* was not a member of a social class but of a profession of considerable importance. This deserves ex- planation, for it throws light on the supernatural element that permeated Maori life. Basically the *tohunga* was a skilled person, an expert in some aspect of work. A *tohunga whaihanga* was an expert in house-building, a *tohunga whakairo* an expert in tattooing, a *tohunga whakairo rakau* an expert in carving. An essential qualification was knowl- edge of the charms and incantations associated with his work and the rituals and religious practices that were essen- tial if the gods were to approve what was done. Because of this the *tohunga* ranked as a priest. It is this function of his profession that is best known to the Pakeha, as it should be, for many *tohunga* were concerned only with the super- natural.

High-born women feeding a tohunga, *the religious leader of the tribe. (National Publicity Studios)*

The *tohunga ahurewa* was the high priest of the cult, trained for years in esoteric lore, skilled in ritual, and possessing mysterious powers denied to those of lesser stature. Then came those whose knowledge and power was confined to the tribal and departmental *atua* (gods). They presided at ceremonies connected with hunting, agriculture, warfare, peacemaking, birth, betrothal, marriage, and death. Their knowledge and skill were essential to the life and prosperity of the tribe. A third class, equally important but less concerned with everyday life, were repositories of genealogies, chants, and knowledge that, in the absence of written records, were enshrined in memory. Together with other

A realistic painting by Gottfried Lindauer of a tohunga *(priest) who is prevented by* tapu *(sacred restriction) from touching cooked food with his hands. (Auckland Art Gallery)*

classes of the priesthood they were required to repeat genealogies, chants, and incantations without pause or mistake for any faltering or error brought swift reprisal from the gods. The lowest type of *tohunga* had dealings with ghosts, demons, evil spirits and local *atua*. Expert in hypnotism and ventriloquism, they were feared as the earthly media of the *atua*, able to exercise control over earthly and unearthly forces. *Makutu* is witchcraft; *kehua* is a ghost, hence they were termed *tohunga ka makutu* and *tohunga kehua*. The supposed proximity of all classes of *tohunga* to the gods, and their supernatural powers, tended to make them natural leaders and advisors in tribal councils.

It is appropriate here to refer to religious and associated concepts evolved during the period that the Maori was separated by distance from other island groups of Polynesia. He brought with him the gods of all the Polynesians. Gradually the *tohunga* wove round them an intricate pattern of changing thought. The fertility of imagination of the Maori, together with his close contact with nature, resulted in an elaboration of mythology that has no parallel elsewhere in Polynesia. New gods were added to the pantheon, in particular **Haumia-tiketike**, whose role was confined to the protection of the rhizome of the bracken. At first sight it may be strange to find a god of such limited interests given equal status with gods of the forest and cultivated food, until we realise that, when all other crops failed, only the almost indigestible, tasteless bracken root provided sustenance throughout the year.

In a very literal sense the Maori lived a god-fearing life. The **wars** of the gods and Tane's valiant ascent of the overworlds to capture the three baskets (*kete o te wananga*) that contained the sum of sacred and occult knowledge, is typical of man's dependence on the gods. The *kete aronui*, the first basket, contained lore relating to the creation of the world, in a greatly expanded form compared with comparative mythologies. Such knowledge was regarded as of supreme importance to mankind. The second basket, the *kete tuauri*, dealt with the practice of ritual and the memorising of invocations and chants. The *kete tuatea* contained *makutu*, or black magic, which proved harmful to mankind.

The famous cycles of legends centred round such gods and demigods as Tawhaki and Maui are elaborations of the fragmentary myths of other parts of Polynesia. Finally, the concepts of natural personifications, giants (typified by Rakaihautu who dug out the deep beds of the southern lakes), *tipua* (the essential supernatural element in enchanted objects), *patupaiarehe* (the tall white-skinned fairy inhabitants of the misty forests), and the monsters known as *taniwha* that inhabit deep pools, are symptomatic of the Maori preoccupation with and dependence on nature.

In everyday life he was at the mercy of the supernatural. Tribal *atua* were primarily war gods, though some had more peaceful characteristics as guardians of domestic arts and cultivation. A few were regarded as more powerful than others and were shared by a number of tribes or sub-tribes. Each god had an *aria* (manifestation) such as the rainbow, thunder, lightning, meteors, comets, stars, or sometimes human beings.

The struggle for territorial rights and the fierce pride of the Maori made him a formidable and often treacherous warrior. A *taua* (war party) on the march would quickly dispatch the first person to cross its path. The victim, whoever he or she might be was "the fish of Tu", a sacrifice to the supreme god of war. On capturing a fortified village, or after a successful ambush, the defeated warriors would be ruthlessly killed, cooked in an earth oven, and eaten at a

An anti-aircraft post of the NZ Pioneer Maori Battalion who served in World War I. (Alexander Turnbull Library)

Among the first troops entering Tripoli in February 1943 were Maoris on their long journey from Alamein. (Alexander Turnbull Library)

cannibal feast, or taken into slavery and subjected to many indignities. The practice of cannibalism can be ascribed to two main causes, the desire to absorb in a literal fashion the *mana* (the strength, power, and influence) of the defeated enemy, and to satisfy hunger. It must be remembered that the only flesh foods that New Zealand could supply were birds, fish, rats, and dogs. There were no native quadrupeds, the rat and the dog having been brought from the homeland.

But in spite of the treachery and vindictiveness of infuriated cannibal warriors, many deeds of chivalry were recorded. Folklore, while heavily laden with tale of warfare, also contains tender love stories such as the immortal legend of Hinemoa who swam across Lake Rotorua in the darkness to join her lover Tutanekai on the island of Mokoia.

Early visitors to New Zealand were fascinated and appalled by the war dance that expressed defiance of the enemy and stimulated the participants to a frenzy. Usually known today as the *haka*, the term was used for many different kinds of dances, and was an important feature of Maori life, an outlet for every kind of emotion. *Haka* were performed on such varied occasions as going to war, making peace, receiving visitors, at birth, death, and marriage ceremonies, greeting the heliacal rising of stars that signalled the beginning of the planting season, and in joy, sorrow, triumph, or derision.

There were slow, graceful dances, others that were fierce and energetic, but all involved the use of head, body and limbs, and were performed standing, sitting, or kneeling. Men and women took part, but the *poi* dance, with fluttering balls of *raupo* down on the end of flax cords, was restricted to women, while the *peruperu*, the proper name for the war dance, was usually though not exclusively performed by men. This posture dance was an outlet for pent-

Maori challenge to the Springbok Rugby team at Ngaruawahia, the home of the Maori King. (National Publicity Studios)

up emotions and an encouragement to the warriors: the eyes and tongues protruded in the defiant *pukana* gesture, the thunder of bare feet on the ground, the rousing song or chant, and the contorted bodies and faces of the dancers were designed to strike fear into the hearts of the enemy. The challenge and the *haka* on the *marae* still remain as part of the traditional reception and welcome to distinguished visitors, who are required to observe the accepted protocol of the occasion.

One of the most famous of all *haka* is that associated with the powerful chief of the Ngati-Toa, Te Rauparaha. He had hidden in a *kumara* pit. As he rises from it he contrasts the darkness of the pit with the rising of the sun.

Ka mate! Ka mate!	It is death! It is death!
Ka ora! Ka ora!	It is life! It is life!
Tenei te tangata puhuruhuru	Here is the hairy man
Nana nei i tiki mai i	Who fetched the sun and
whakawhiti te ra,	caused it to shine again,
Hupane! Kaupane!	Hupane! Kaupane!
Whiti te ra!	The sun shines!

The dance has its origin in a phenomenon of nature, for the *haka* is the embodiment of the dance of Tane-rore, the personified form of quivering, heated air of summer, the child of Te Ra, the sun god, and Hine-raumati, the summer girl.

Despite internecine warfare, the Maori travelled widely throughout both islands. Inland tribes bartered preserved eels, vegetable food, and forest birds for the sea fish of coastal tribes. Raiding parties made use of narrow bush tracks, or travelled in huge war canoes to attack their enemies. Long distances were covered by canoe. The preponderance of population was in the North Island, but voyages to the South Island were made for supplies of precious greenstone, either from the deposits on the west coast or by barter with the local tribes.

Villages ranged in size from a few individual dwellings to the larger *pa* such as that on One Tree Hill in Auckland. The fertile Tamaki isthmus provided ample food supplies for the people of Maungakiekie, 5,000 strong, as the many terraces that can still be seen on the slopes of the mountain bear testimony.

A large Maori war canoe, fully manned, at the centenary of the signing of the Treaty of Waitangi in 1940. (Alexander Turnbull Library)

Few people occupied the South Island, where the weaker tribes had been driven by invaders of the north. The Ngati-Mamoe, for instance, were forced far south by the stronger Ngai-Tahu tribe, which had in turn been driven out of the North Island. The Ngati-Mamoe took refuge in the almost impregnable fastnesses of Fiordland, where they later became known as the Lost Tribe. A single family was discovered in Dusky Sound by Captain Cook on his second voyage (1773), and there were later rumours of voices in the dense forests, but no definite sightings of the Lost Tribe have been made since Cook's day.

Women are still engaged in the age-old craft of weaving flax leaves into baskets. The centre panel in the background portrays the fabulous bird-woman Kurangaitaku of Rotorua. (Fritz Prenzel)

A guide stands beside a carved figure holding a representation of a mere pounamu *(greenstone club) at Whakarewarewa, Rotorua. (Fritz Prenzel)*

CHAPTER 4

MATERIAL CULTURE

*He tangata momoe, he tangata mangere, e kore e
whiwhi ki te taonga.*
A sleepy man, a lazy man, will never acquire possessions.

THE PROVERB reminds us that the hours of every day
were occupied with warfare or peaceful pursuits that required unremitting toil, occasionally interspersed with
gargantuan feasts and entertainments. The Maori was wonderfully hospitable, and improvidently generous. When
visitors arrived, food stores were opened and the guests
entertained so lavishly that months of semi-starvation might
follow for the hosts. The evenings were usually times of
relaxation, enlivened by song and dance, and the retelling
of old legends and local gossip until the open hearth fires
died down and old and young composed themselves for
sleep on their *whariki* (floor mats). Only the sentries remained alert on the watchtower to guard against a surprise
attack.

Everyday life may well be illustrated by a brief descrip-
tion of the material culture and artifacts of the old-time
Maori.

The Whare. Most of the buildings in the *pa* were low
and small. The largest and most imposing was the meeting
house with thatched roof, carved posts and bargeboards,
and wall panels interspersed with screens of woven reed
and pampas grass stems. A wide verandah, frequently used
during wet weather, fronted the meeting house, which had

a single door and window. The rafters were painted red, white, and brown in traditional patterns. Open fireplaces were placed inside to provide warmth and light, but the absence of chimneys made the interior smoky and over-heated, especially when the meeting house was used for songs, dances and speechmaking. The most outstanding feature of the houses was the huge carvings that supported the posts, the front one being crowned with a human effigy termed a *tekoteko*. The grotesque or, if one appreciates this form of art, the conventionalised figure carvings, were those of famous ancestors.

The *whare* (houses) had no furniture except for the

Beautifully carved Maori house in the National (formerly Dominion) Museum, Wellington. (National Publicity Studios)

sleeping mats, which were folded up during the day. Meals were invariably eaten outside, for food was destructive of *tapu*, and could not be cooked or eaten inside. If we could conjure up the scene at night when everyone crowded into the meeting house, we would see dark-skinned heavily tattooed faces lit by the flickering flames of the fires, the light gleaming on the dancers' polished skins. The young women would sing, dancing to the rhythm of the song, their *poi* balls fluttering in their hands like the flight of the lively fantail bird. Perhaps an old chieftainess with wrinkled face, chin and lips tattooed with blue pigment, would tell one of the hero-stories of the tribe. Everyone would then

Maori guide explains carving to tourists at the Ohinemutu Meeting House, Rotorua. (National Publicity Studios)

fall quiet, following the tale critically to ensure that no variants were introduced into stories that were hallowed by tradition. Or perhaps one of the *rangatira* would stride up and down the aisle, his greenstone club quivering in his hand, urging the young men to take revenge for some real or fancied insult to the tribe. It would be a call for *utu*, the word that denotes payment for injury. (In modern times it was anglicised to "hoot".)

Clothing. Men and women wore the same simple garments—a kilt or apron fastened by a belt, and a cloak—a square of woven flax fibre tied across the shoulders but discarded when working. The cloaks were woven by the women in a manner unknown to other Polynesian people, who fashioned them from *tapa* cloth. The Maori relied on the ubiquitous flax fibre. Two or four sticks were placed upright in the ground, then the fibre, scraped from the green leaves of the flax plant and treated until it was as bright and glossy as spun silk, was rolled into thread and woven between the sticks. It took months to make a cloak, but the finished article was a thing of beauty and greatly prized. The most valuable cloaks were edged with threads dyed red and black, woven into geometric patterns; finally they were further decorated with tufts of feathers or dogs' hair.

For ornaments there were greenstone ear and neck pendants. The *tiki* or, more correctly, the *hei tiki*, suspended from a cord round the neck, was the most prized possession of the *rangatira*. It has been surmised that this little amulet was a symbol of fertility, carved in the form of a human foetus, but the plain truth is that the tilted head, compressed arms, and folded legs were easier to carve and less likely to suffer damage than an image with protrusions. Discarded adze blades lent themselves to this treatment, and were

Aged Maori woman at Rotorua. (K. & J. Bigwood)

A Maori greenstone, hei tiki, *most prized possession of a rangatira. (National Publicity Studios)*

often used for the purpose. The fact that many of these prized heirlooms have survived intact for hundreds of years proves the wisdom of the carvers in keeping the design as simple as possible. As the hard greenstone required months of patient work before the ornament was completed, it is no wonder that the images were so greatly treasured. *Rangatira* wore the black, white-tipped feathers of the now extinct *huia* bird in the hair, which was drawn into a top-knot. Women allowed theirs to flow loosely.

The most distinctive of all ornamentation, however, was the *moko* or facial tattoo. The earliest arrivals in Aotearoa knew nothing of the elaborate art form that later developed. It was a long and painful process, for the design was

Early drawing of tattooed Maori chief with top knot (putiki wharanui). *(National Publicity Studios)*

literally carved into the skin by means of a small bone chisel and mallet, the grooves being filled with indelible pigment. Only a small part of the design could be completed at one time, for the wound had to heal before the work could be continued. A man could not claim to be fully tattooed until his entire face was covered, and often his buttocks as well. Women, either married or single, were tattooed only on lips and chin. Tattooing had no social or other significance. It appears to have been purely decorative in its intent, and was closely allied to the art of woodcarving. The practice died out during the early twentieth century, but at the time of writing (1973) there are a few very old *kuia* (old ladies) still living who proudly carry the *moko* on lips and chin.

A richly carved and decorated pulpit in a church at Kawhia shows how effectively the geometric patterns of reeds and toetoe stems can be employed.

An adaptation of traditional carving to modern use at Taupo. The supporting posts in the form of human figures illustrate a posture of the war dance.

Woodcarving. Many books and articles have been written on this fascinating subject. In the present survey the photographs reproduced in this book are more eloquent than words. Throughout Polynesia there are many outstanding examples of woodcarving, but none to compare with the accomplishments of the New Zealand Maori. There are two obvious reasons for this and a third that is more subtle and possibly debatable—the Maori genius for personification and his intimacy with the natural world in which he lived.

Firstly, in the *totara* New Zealand possesses timber that is ideally suited to the purpose—straight-grained, easily worked, and durable, while the northern *kauri* tree also provides ideal timber for the largest war canoes. Secondly, greenstone—hard, durable and capable of taking a keen edge—provided adzes and chisels that did all the carving experts could ask for, and more. Months and even years of work might go into the making and polishing of these tools, but the final result was an implement that could work magic in the hands of craftsmen.

It is not to be supposed that the art flowered immediately the first Polynesians came to Aotearoa. Ancient carvings are markedly different in style, as are the products of the carvers in different parts of New Zealand. One striking difference between the carvings of the Maori and those of other island groups lies in its curvilinear form. Seen at its most delicate and lacelike form in the double spirals of the bow and stern pieces of a war canoe, and on weapons, musical instruments, and *waka huia* (the oval caskets in which heirlooms were stored), this remarkable dexterity of the carver has no parallel elsewhere in Polynesia. In spite of the formalised patterns, natural beauty is seen in many forms. It has been suggested that the spiral design with its incised surface patterns may be in imitation of the unfolding fernfrond. Larger sculptures and smaller objects, carved in high relief, frequently depict the stylised human form. In modern terminology, the work is always functional as well as decorative, the face or figure being adapted to the proper use and purpose of the object, whether it be a flute, the handle of a club, or the sturdy centre post or wall slab of a meeting house.

An interesting development was the *manaia*, which has been variously interpreted as a bird-headed man, a representation of the *mana* or spiritual power of man, or a bird that attacks man. A recent theory is that it represents the human head in profile. If two *manaia* are placed side by side, the

Ornately carved wooden vessel used for holding liquid, in National Museum, Wellington. (National Publicity Studios)

A waka huia, *a carved bowl used for storing the highly prized huia feather. (National Publicity Studios)*

Modern Maori carver at work at Whakarewarewa, Rotorua. (National Publicity Studios)

full face is seen. A considerable degree of ingenuity was shown in the adaptation of the *manaia* to fit spaces in the most intricate carvings.

Fortunately the ancient art of Maori carving has not been lost. Working with steel tools in place of greenstone adzes and chisels, the Maori craftsman of today still produces a variety of truly traditional work ranging from tourist souvenirs to the massive figures that are such an outstanding feature of large meeting houses. The gigantic pillar carved by the late Inia te Wiata and displayed in New Zealand House, London, is an outstanding example of the work of a dedicated twentieth-century carver.

Weapons. The Maori was an in-fighter, delighting in hand-to-hand combat. Boys were trained in throwing long reed darts, but in manhood a slender bone-tipped spear, sometimes eight or nine metres in length, was used only in hunting birds. True, he possessed a throwing spear for use in warfare, usually to penetrate the defensive palisades of a *pa*, but he trusted his life to his skill with *patu* and *taiaha*. The *patu* was a club, of which there were several varieties. The favourite *patu* was the *mere*, a thin-bladed club, the handle being attached to the wrist by a leather thong. Frequently made of greenstone (*pounamu*), a well-made *mere* could deal a stunning blow or lift the top of a man's skull by a thrust to the temple and a quick turn of the wrist. The *taiaha*, described as a quarter-staff, was a chiefly weapon. Made of straight-grained, hard, springy *manuka* or tea-tree, it was light and strong. The butt broadened into a flattened end, the point was carved in the semblance of an out-thrust tongue, decorated with a bunch of feathers. The striking point would dart at an enemy's head, the feathers fluttering and confusing him; then the butt would be swung over with stunning impact.

A number of other weapons made of wood, bone, or stone were also used with deadly effect, but none was prized

Carved Maori wahaika, *or wooden club, used in hand-to-hand fighting. (National Publicity Studios)*

Native pigeon, much sought after by the ancient Maoris for eating.
(National Publicity Studios)

and handed from one generation to the next as were the *mere* and the *taiaha*.

Implements. The tools connected with various occupations were mostly related to the gathering and preparation of food. In the plantation men used the *ko* or digging stick, a long pole with a step, to turn over the furrows, working rhythmically to an appropriate chant. When the ground was turned over the women followed, breaking up the soil with wooden clubs, and picking out the weeds. Because of *tapu* restrictions, they were not allowed to plant the seed *kumara*, but were expected to pick caterpillars off the growing plants.

The *hue* or gourd plant was cultivated to provide bowls and jars, for the art of pottery was unknown to the Maori.

Forest birds provided a staple article of diet. Skilled hunters speared them in trees or captured them in snares. The forest provided much of their food. Flightless birds, such as the nocturnal *kiwi*, and rats, were caught in ground snares. Pigeons were captured in nooses set round wooden water troughs and in trees. Wood-hens, naturally inquisitive were attracted by various means and snared on a noose at the end of a long pole. The noisy *kaka*, which could break the cords of a snare with his strong beak, was lured towards the hunter by means of a decoy bird and captured by hand, or speared.

In rivers and streams eels also were speared, or caught by hand, in nets, or taken with a bob. Where they were in plentiful supply in running water, large weirs were constructed by driving posts deep into the bed of the river and interlacing them with brushwood. Eel-pots of woven stems were placed at the outlet and the eels removed from a door in the side of the pot.

A great deal of skill was shown in the manufacture of fish hooks, which were made of bone, wood, shell, or stone. Fish and shellfish were used for bait, with feathers, or slivers of iridescent *paua* shell, as lures. The barbs were either an integral part of the hook or lashed in place, usually with the barb on the inside. Large wooden hooks, sometimes inset with dogs' teeth, were used to catch sharks, barracouta, kingfish, and *kahawai*. Gouges were also employed in sea fishing; the slivers of bone, pointed at both ends and attached to a cord at the centre, were buried in the bait. When the line was pulled the gouge swung sideways to prevent the fish from escaping.

An old legend tells how the chief Kahukura had a recurring dream of some mysterious object called a *kupenga* that would enable his people to catch many fish at a time. He tramped overland to Doubtless Bay and saw the *turehu*, the sea fairies, catching fish by means of a net. Mingling with them, he gained possession of the net by a stratagem and so introduced the seine net to his fellow countrymen.

The making of seine nets was a community activity. Sinkers of stones were placed in coarse woven bags. Light

A far cry from ancient methods: Maori fishermen land a catch at Gisborne. (National Publicity Studios)

whau wood was used for floats. Except at the dedication of a new net, women assisted in hauling the net ashore and gathering up the fish. Some of the nets were of enormous size, the largest being more than a kilometre in length. In addition to the seine nets, smaller hand nets of several kinds were used for taking shrimps, whitebait, and small fish.

Canoes. Although the double canoes, or single ones with an outrigger, brought the Polynesians to New Zealand, a new development soon took place. The tall *totara* and *kauri* trees enabled the Maori to build long, deep canoes that required only a single topstrake and did not need an out-rigger for stability. Many of the locally built canoes were more than twenty metres in length and two in width. Thwarts lashed across the larger canoes served to strengthen them. The decking was made of long rods, with spaces for bailing. When sails were employed they were in the form of inverted triangles.

Small, unornamented canoes were constantly in use on rivers and lakes, larger ones in deep-sea fishing. The *waka taua*, the war canoe, was a work of art with its tall carved stern piece and defiant prow. It was frequently made in three parts—a large middle-section hollowed from a single tree trunk, with separate bow and stern attached with a carefully fitted mortice-and-tenon joint. The paddles were graceful objects, the flattened blades tapering to a point. The average size was a little under two metres. Steering paddles were larger, and frequently had the *manaia* design carved at the end of the handle.

Food. Kumara, vegetable food, and fish and birds (and on occasion human flesh) were cooked in *hangi* (earth ovens). On special social occasions food is still commonly cooked in this way. A fire was lit at the bottom of a pit to heat a layer of stones piled on the flames. Layers of leaves and branches were placed below and above the food, water sprinkled on them to create steam, and a covering of mats laid on top, with earth heaped over. The cooking time was about two hours.

Plates or pots were not available, shallow flax baskets being woven to hold the food when it was cooked.

Recreation. The long evening hours and wet days were occupied with games such as *whai* (cat's cradle) and *ti rakau*, the famous "stick game" in which wooden rods are tossed from player to player to the rhythm of a song. Riddles and

Large Maori war canoe in the Auckland Museum. (National Publicity Studios)

hand games were also popular. Outdoor sports were enjoyed for their own sake by young and old. Whip and humming-tops, tobogganing, kite-flying, and walking on stilts were popular with all ages. In many villages the *moari*, usually termed a giant stride, was erected close to a pond or river. The players swung round at the end of ropes and dropped feet first into the water. River and sea sports—swimming, racing in small canoes, and surfing—were good training for the time when men went to war in the *waka taua* and for women who gathered shellfish and lobsters. The dexterity achieved in every kind of outdoor sport was of the utmost importance in the training of warriors.

Maori woman weaving the border for a cloak. (National Publicity Studios)

CHAPTER 5

THE COMING OF THE PAKEHA

Kua u mai tenei tauhou,
ki tenei whenua tauhou.
This stranger has arrived at a strange land.

OUT OF the empty seas came two white-winged canoes.
The year was 1642, the "canoes" the vessels *Zeehaen* and
Heemskirk, under the command of the Dutch navigator
Abel Janszoon Tasman. He sighted the snow-clad peaks of
the Southern Alps and the rocky west coast of the South
Island, turned northwards, rounded Farewell Spit and
anchored in Tasman Bay. The first contact of the representatives of two different cultures was disastrous, for both
Maori and Pakeha were killed on that day. Leaving his fate-
ful anchorage Tasman sailed northwards, sighted the men of
another tribe on the Three Kings Islands, and disappeared,
his impact scarcely more palpable than the wake of his ships
on the sea.

Nevertheless a straggling line on the world map would in-
dicate henceforth the presence of a land which Tasman
believed to be part of a Great Southern Continent. More
than a century passed before another canoe with white
sails came in sight of New Zealand. Captain James Cook in
the bark *Endeavour* made his first landing at Turanga, the
site of the present city of Gisborne. The tale of his adven-
tures as he circumnavigated both islands is one that lies
beyond the confines of the present book, except for his
contacts with the Maori people. There were occasional skir-

mishes, but Cook was a humane man, intensely interested
in the inhabitants of the country, and a keen observer of
their life and customs. His journal[1] provides an invaluable
record of Maori life before it was changed by contact with
Europeans.

His visit had two immediate consequences. It soon became known in Europe that the southern parts of the South
Island abounded in seals. Before the end of the century
sealing gangs were put ashore and, inevitably, took Maori
wives who were a comfort to men living in such a lonely,
demanding situation for months at a time. The second
mingling of the two races occurred at the north of the
North Island, at the Bay of Islands, which became a rendez-
vous for whaling vessels. At one fell swoop the Maori of the
Nga-Puhi tribe was introduced to the vices of a so-called
civilisation. The chiefs were not slow to take advantage of
the benefits offered by women-hungry whaling men ripe
for any excitement ashore while the ships' stores were being
replenished. The Maoris at the Bay became accustomed to
the white men and their needs. As their experience grew
they traded potatoes and pork for blankets and tools, muskets and gunpowder. In many cases, unfortunately, they
succumbed to the sailors' vices, and were vulnerable to their
diseases. Increasing contact resulted in widespread epi-
demics that took a dreadful toll of their numbers in the
latter part of the eighteenth and for long into the nineteenth
century.

There are two aspects to the early contacts: one the impact on the Maori of sealers, whalers and an occasional flax
and timber trader; the other the reaction of the Maori to
the increasing number of visitors. A warrior race was naturally impressed by the efficacy of the musket as a weapon.
In a short space of time a vigorous trade sprang up, pro-

Captain Cook landing at Poverty Bay. The Endeavour in background. Mural by P. Read. (National Publicity Studios)

Maori social life and customs. A family group about 1890. (Alexander Turnbull Library, Head Collection)

visions and flax being bartered for muskets and powder. This had a profound effect on life wherever tribal lands were contiguous with white settlement or visitation. Vast quantities of flax fibre were needed for the purchase of a single musket. In consequence many healthy *kainga* and hill *pa* were abandoned while the tribes lived for months in swampy land gathering and scraping the flax. These unhealthy conditions contributed substantially to the ravages of tuberculosis and other European diseases. The Maori was placed in an invidious position. Unless he accumulated a sufficient arsenal of the Pakeha's weapons he would be at the mercy of better-equipped tribes, yet the only way to prevent this was to engage in ceaseless toil in unhealthy localities.

And again, there was a twofold consequence of the new regime. Tribal warfare assumed new and more deadly proportions, and also led to a truculent attitude towards the Pakeha. This in itself was inevitable. It was intensified by the possession of firearms—but natural ferocity and primitive weapons were also responsible for the majority of attacks on unwary or ill-equipped Pakehas.

For the first few decades of the nineteenth century acts of bloodshed were commonplace, especially in the North Island. In Australia interest in New Zealand was increasing rapidly, but in 1809, when the crew of the *Boyd* was killed and the vessel destroyed in Whangaroa Harbour, interest tended to evaporate. The incident is usually referred to as the *Boyd* "massacre", a term that comes, or used to come, lightly to the lips of the Pakeha.

By this time many young Maoris had taken service in whaling vessels, either through natural curiosity or being shanghaied by unscrupulous captains. Some were abandoned in distant ports. Eventually many returned. Among them was a young Whangaroa chief who had served on the *Boyd*. During the voyage he had been flogged on the captain's orders. This was an indignity that cried out for revenge and—in Maori fashion—the insult was wiped out with finality. But whaling crews at the Bay of Islands were equally ready for revenge and set out on a punitive expedition. Unfortunately, through a similarity of names, they attacked a tribe whose chief had been noted for his friendship to the Pakeha. The twofold "massacre" put an end to amicable relations and postponed for five years the arrival of the first white missionaries.

A Christmas service at Oihi in the Bay was the next significant step in the meeting of the two cultures. The Rev Samuel Marsden, Chaplain of New South Wales, had for

Hongi Hika, 1777-1828, the noted Maori chief. A sketch by Robley from a painting by Barry. (Alexander Turnbull Library)

some time been befriending stranded Maori sailors in Sydney. Though never a resident missionary in New Zealand, he was responsible for the establishment of the Church Missionary Society there, and on his first Christmas Day service in the Bay he was assisted by Ruatara, a young chief who, before his untimely death, did much to promote the work of the Church.

Marsden's policy, viewed with the perspective of a century and a half, can still be regarded as both humanitarian and statesmanlike, for he considered that training in agricultural and other peaceful arts was a necessary prelude to conversion. Everywhere he went during his many visits to New Zealand, he was treated with respect and affection. Te Matenga, as he was known, was the acknowledged friend of the Maori people. He proved to be a peacemaker as well as an evangelist.

With few exceptions the resident missionaries, lay and clerical, had a much more difficult time. Living in primitive conditions, unable because of their convictions to offer muskets in return for provisions, and separated by distance from all but occasional contacts with their headquarters, they were surrounded by difficulties and were often in fear of their lives. Following Marsden's instructions, they attempted to introduce western methods of agriculture, taught reading and writing, and endeavoured by example as well as precept to soften the hearts of a warlike race. They were slow to make conversions, or at least to accept converts for baptism—a policy that had much to justify it, and that ultimately proved successful.

Meanwhile the supply of firearms grew, at first steadily and then with a rush after a powerful northern chief, Hongi Hika, had been taken to England by one of the missionaries. The purpose of the visit was to enable the Maori language to be studied and printed on accepted linguistic principles. Hongi was introduced to King George IV and presented with a suit of armour and a number of other valuable presents. At Sydney he exchanged most of the gifts for powder and muskets, and so was able to equip the Nga-Puhi tribe with formidable fire-power. He lost little time in subjugating less fortunate tribes as far south as Tauranga and Rotorua. The scenes of carnage were indescribable. Many were the canoes that returned to the Bay laden with a living cargo of men, women, and children reduced to servitude or destined to provide food for endless cannibal feasts. If it had not been for the influence of the missionaries, the slaughter would doubtless have been much greater.

Time was the inevitable victor. Hongi died of a wound. The fires of battle were reduced, even though they were not yet quenched. Gradually missionary influence prevailed. Converted chiefs released many slaves who returned to their own tribes, helping to spread the message of the white man's Gospel. Everywhere the Maori people were anxious to learn to read, and portions of the Bible, translated into their own language, were as eagerly sought after as muskets.

It must not, of course, be thought that New Zealand became a land of peace and plenty, either then or later. Another warrior, Te Rauparaha, fearful of attack by the powerful Waikato tribes, led his people, the Ngati-Toa, southwards from Kawhia, and occupied the island of Kapiti and the adjacent mainland. A ruthless and farsighted strategist, he exterminated the local tribes, extended his raids to the South Island, and established what appeared to be friendly relations with the first-comers among the Pakeha in his district. Later he became a menace to European occupation.

Meanwhile the tide of white settlement was swelling steadily, though almost imperceptibly. The British Government, mindful of its problems with the colonists in America and the difficulty of administering the convict settlement in New South Wales, was not anxious to add to its burdens. Captain Cook had claimed the country as a British possession, but the Imperial Government remained aloof. This studied indifference could not be sustained. Increasing numbers of settlers, missionaries, traders, agriculturalists, and those who were purchasing Maori land, resulted in demands for protection; on the other hand, if Britain did did not step in and offer the protection to which all British subjects were then entitled, it would be an open invitation to other nations to acquire further overseas possessions.

London's first reluctant step was to place New Zealand under the jurisdiction of the Governor of New South Wales, who appointed a "British Resident" to the Bay of Islands. Lacking definite powers and an armed force, James Busby, who had accepted the appointment, could do little or nothing to keep either the turbulent Maoris or the roistering whaling crews in order.

Yet another event forced London to act. The formation there of the powerful New Zealand Association, established to promote settlement on a systematically planned basis, resulted in the lobbying of members of Parliament, and a threat of usurpation of government authority.

It may be thought that these movements have little to do with the Maori people, but it was from such beginnings that events in New Zealand developed so dramatically. Until 1840 there were many contacts between Maori and Pakeha with action and reaction affecting Maori life; but in that year occurred an event that was destined to shape the future of a race that had been in total and undisputed possession of their land for hundreds of years.

In January 1840 Captain William Hobson arrived at the Bay of Islands. Great Britain had at length decided to proclaim New Zealand a Crown Colony and, after annexation, to appoint a Lieutenant-Governor to safeguard the interests of the Queen's subjects, both Maori and Pakeha. But first the Maoris were required to sign a treaty that would place themselves and their land under the protection of the Great White Queen.

The Treaty of Waitangi is a landmark not only in New Zealand history but also in the history of nineteenth-

A version of the signing of the Treaty of Waitangi, by L.C. Mitchell. (National Publicity Studios)

century colonial expansion. It emphasised three important conditions:

1. The chiefs were required to acknowledge the Queen of England as their ruler (a difficult concept for a multitude of tribal chiefs who acknowledged no one overlord).

2. The tribes were to be allowed to retain possession of their land but, in anticipation of sales, it was stipulated that for the protection of the vendors, such sales should be made only to the Crown.

3. The right and privileges of British citizenship were to be enjoyed by the Maori people.

"*He iwi tahi tatou,*" Hobson said to the assembled chiefs. "We are now one people."

After some initial and well-justified reluctance, a number of chiefs signed the Treaty and Hobson formally accepted the office of Governor. Subsequently copies of the Treaty were circulated throughout the country. Further signatures were obtained, though it should be noted that some powerful chiefs, of whom Te Heuheu of Ngati-Tuwharetoa was one, refused to sign.

The clauses relating to land sales were vital to both parties. To the Governor, the officials, the land speculators (who were alarmed at the prospect of pre-emption to the Crown), and doubtless to the missionaries, the issue was crystal clear.

From the Maori point of view, it was far from clear. Despite the efforts of the missionaries (who were opposed to extensive colonisation) to explain the purpose and meaning of the Treaty, it was obviously impossible to convey European concepts to those who regarded land not as a commodity but as a sacred gift of Tane, a heritage passed down from the tribal ancestors or fairly won in bloody

84

combat, a possession that could never be sold, bartered or alienated.

It must be admitted that on occasion the Maori was more wily than the land-grabbing Pakeha. There were occasions when the same land was sold many times over; but even in such cases the Maori did not fully realise that his land would be lost in perpetuity, but rather believed that its occupation was being granted for a limited period, eventually to be returned to its rightful owners.

References. 1. *Captain Cook in New Zealand.* Edited by A.H. and A.W. Reed. A.H. & A.W. Reed Ltd.

CHAPTER 6

CONFLICT OF CULTURES

*Ka tahuna te ururua ki te ahi e kore e tumau tonu ki
te wahi i tahuna atu ai; kaore ka ka katoa te parae.*

When the bush is set on fire, the flames will not remain
there in the dry brushwood; no, they will spread over the plains.

CONTEMPORANEOUSLY with official annexation, the first New Zealand Company settlers began to arrive at Port Nicholson, the future port of Wellington. Their need for large areas of land was urgent; the method of purchase was in direct violation of the principles laid down for the guidance of the Governor. At Port Nicholson the local Maoris sold their land for a varied assortment of cash and goods, ranging from blankets and nightcaps to jew's harps. The leader of the settlement, Colonel Wakefield, ranged far afield beyond the range of Wellington's encircling hills in an endeavour to acquire land for farming. Time and again the Maoris scrambled to secure a few handfuls of the Pakeha treasure, no matter how useless it might be. The seeds of immediate confrontation with the government and future trouble with the Maoris were broadcast with a liberal hand.

In the beginning, however, there was cordiality between Maori and settler. From the Maori viewpoint, the arrival of a few Pakehas increased local *mana* and provided a source of income, for Maori help was needed to build temporary *raupo whares* to house the settlers and their families. The Maori's ancestral domain, the larder provided by Tane, he imagined to be still securely in his possession.

It was not long before he realised that, in Biblical terms, he had sold his inheritance for a mess of pottage. The stream of newcomers became a flood. They demanded more and yet more land. Settlements were established at Wanganui and Taranaki, and at Nelson in the South Island. Trees were felled without propitiation to the gods. Whole forests were being swept away. The *mana* of the white man was swallowing up the *mana* the Maori.

The first open conflict occurred in the South Island. To understand its origin we must go back to the advent of Te Rauparaha, the wily Ngati-Toa chief and his equally blood-thirsty nephew Te Rangihaeata. After practically extermi-nating the Muaupoko tribe and settling at Kapiti Island and Waikanae, Te Rauparaha conducted a number of raids across Cook Strait, notably against the large *pa* at Kaiapohia (Kaiapoi) and at Akaroa. As a byproduct of these sangui-nary victories he claimed ownership of the Wairau Valley in Marlborough. He made no attempt to settle there, but nevertheless it belonged to his people by right of conquest. When an early whaler, John Blenkinsopp, married one of Te Rauparaha's relatives, he was permitted to "purchase" the valley by gift of a ship's cannon, and a deed of sale was executed. The years passed by. The Ngati-Toa chief may well have forgotten the transaction; even if he remembered, it may be taken for granted that he had no intention of allowing the land to be alienated by a crowd of land-hungry settlers. But the deed of sale had been purchased by the New Zealand Company for £300. Their officials under-standably regarded it as proof of their ownership of the fertile valley.

The scene now shifts to Nelson, where Captain Arthur Wakefield, the leader of the settlement, was in dire need of more land to allow the settlers to take up their country

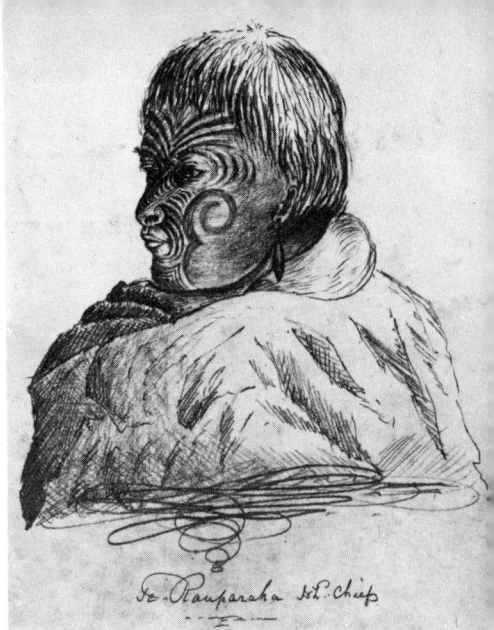

Pencil sketch by Charles Heaphy of Te Rauparaha, the famous Maori chief. (Alexander Turnbull Library, W.F. Airey)

allotments. Surveyors were sent to the Wairau. They met a party of Maoris headed by Te Rauparaha and Te Rangihaeata, who promptly pulled up the survey pegs and burnt the surveyors' makeshift *whare*. When the news reached Nelson, Captain Wakefield assembled a posse and accompanied the men to the Wairau to assert his rights. The confrontation was disastrous. On the banks of the Tua Marina stream a shot was fired, probably by an excited settler, and in the resulting skirmish a number of deaths occurred on both sides, among them a wife of Te Rangihaeata, and Colonel Wakefield. It is significant that what in earlier years was termed the Wairau Massacre is now referred to as the Wairau Affair or Affray—significant because it is now realised that there was right and reason on both sides.

Some time later a newly-appointed Governor, Robert FitzRoy, upheld the Maori ownership, to the great indig-

nation of the settlers, and probably much to the surprise of
the Maoris, who regarded it as a sign of weakness rather
than justice on the part of the Pakeha.

Important as this incident was to the settlers of the New
Zealand Company, it had wider implications. The Ngati-Toa
chiefs became emboldened to take the offensive, and the
settlement at Wellington was threatened. Several brief
engagements between Maori warriors and British troops
took place in the Hutt and Horokiwi valleys. Had it not
been for the moderating influence of the Rev Octavius
Hadfield, the CMS missionary at Otaki, it is almost certain
that the Wellington settlers would have been overwhelmed.

The days of comparative security were over. To use the
old Maori phrase, the "fire in the fern" spread to the Bay of
Islands. Hone Heke, who had been instrumental in persu-
ading other chiefs to sign the Treaty, had become disil-
lusioned. Until 1841 Kororareka (present-day Russell) was
New Zealand's capital and its busiest port, and a lucrative
trade had developed, to the benefit of the powerful Nga-
Puhi tribe. When the capital was shifted to Auckland, trade
declined. All that remained were the tattered remnants of a
new way of life that had replaced the centuries-old customs
of a proud race of people. These and other factors drove
Hone Heke and another powerful chief, Kawiti, to open
rebellion. The flagstaff on Maiki Hill, the Pakeha symbol of
authority, was cut down, not once but four times, and
eventually the township of Kororareka was attacked and
burnt. As usual, the Maori warriors displayed many acts of
chivalry. Homeless people were allowed to take refuge on
ships.

The alarm that spread in the infant township of Auckland
on the arrival of the refugees can be imagined. More Imperial
troops were brought from Australia, and the War in the

Lieutenant Te Moana-nui-a-Kiwa won a posthumous VC for magnificent courage in World War II. (Alexander Turnbull Library)

North, as it is usually called, began. For some time Heke and Kawiti had the best of it. The British forces were unused to the kind of fighting in which the Maori excelled. When a *pa* was assailed by superior force, including the use of artillery, the defenders simply evacuated it, after having inflicted heavy losses on the attackers, and took up another position.

Their greatest danger came from Maoris who supported the British forces. In later wars, also, the support of some tribes was an important factor in the success of British soldiers and settlers. In the War in the North it was not until a hastily-appointed Governor, Sir George Grey, took office that the tide turned against Heke and Kawiti. Their final defeat was at Tuapekapeka (Cave of the Bat). The end was hastened by an attack on a Sunday morning, a day on which, because of missionary teaching, the Maoris had expected that all fighting would cease.

Fortunately Sir George Grey had great respect and admiration for the Maori people and Heke and Kawiti were treated with clemency.

Except for occasional outbursts and a growing sense of unease amongst their leaders, the position of the tribes during the next ten to fifteen years was relatively satisfactory. For a time it seemed that a balance between Pakeha aggressiveness and Maori acceptance of a new way of life had been reached. This was particularly the case in the Auckland province, and also in the South Island, where the Maori population was small and where Pakeha settlement took place much later than in the North Island.

As a result of missionary influence a large proportion of the Maori population had embraced Christianity. By 1856 their eagerness to read the Scriptures resulted in an astonishing situation in which the proportion of Maoris who could read and write was greater than that of the Europeans living in New Zealand. The Maoris no longer depended on hunting and fishing for their food supplies. They assisted the settlers to clear the bush from their allotments, built their houses, and grew food for them. Large areas of land were sown with wheat and potatoes. In the towns Maoris bartered pigs and kits of potatoes and peaches brought by canoe or carried overland. Owing largely to missionary encouragement they possessed flourmills and trading schooners. By 1855 most of the coastal shipping trade was under Maori ownership. Fifty per cent of the country's exports was supplied by Maoris, who paid half the total customs revenue. A subsistence economy had been replaced by a thriving agricultural and trading industry.

John Gorst, a magistrate in the prosperous Waikato district, wrote that "in reasoning especially on political topics, in making provision for their own Government, and for the education of their children, they exhibited unexpected cleverness and good sense. There were at that time numerous village schools . . . founded and managed entirely by the natives themselves . . . The girls wore clean print frocks; the boys blue cotton shirts and duck trousers. The pupils could invariably answer simple questions on religion, read their own language well and in some schools showed a knowledge of arithmetic that filled me with surprise."

This pleasant picture of a happy, contented, apparently independent race conforming to the standards of the Pakeha invader was not destined to survive. Within a few years the Pakeha outnumbered the Maori, and the tide of settlers showed no signs of diminishing. The infant, unwanted colony had grown in strength and had been granted political independence. The Government and the Provincial councils were in practice if not in theory the representatives only of the Pakeha. Hunger for land and yet more land could not be appeased, and control of land sales varied according to the political climate. The pressure to sell was unrelenting. The more thoughtful chiefs were becoming seriously concerned, not only on account of the loss of land, but also because of the degradation of many of their people who could not resist the lure of ready money, tobacco, and alcohol. For the first time they resolved their differences in an attempt to protect their tribal lands. The movement gained in strength in Waikato and Taranaki. The obvious solution was to appoint a King who could speak for all the Maori people, or at least for those tribes which were prepared to give him their allegiance.

The final choice fell to the Waikato chief Potatau te

Wherowhero, on account of his *mana* and illustrious descent. The principle of *kotahitanga*, of oneness or unity. was born.

Parliamentarians were alarmed at the formation of what they regarded as a seditious movement and at the outspoken threats of the more turbulent chiefs to drive the Pakeha into the sea. Cases of harassment and murder of settlers on isolated farms created an alarm that reached a crisis at Waitara in Taranaki.

The Government had bought land in this district from a chief who claimed that he had the right to sell. The sale was contested by Wiremu Kingi, who tried to persuade the Government to cancel the sale and restore it to its rightful owners—not to an individual but to the tribe. His request was refused, ill-advisedly, and martial law was proclaimed in New Plymouth. It is worthy of note that, after much bloodshed, the validity of Kingi's claim was eventually recognised and compensation paid to the Taranaki tribes.

The conflict there was but the opening of a more extensive war that escalated into Waikato and the Bay of Plenty. The Maori warriors pitted their skill against the combined forces of regular Imperial troops, volunteer combat units, and an ill-trained militia. Resourceful and skilled as the Maori proved to be in bush fighting, the end was inevitable. The war in the Waikato ended tragically yet splendidly. The Maori King's stronghold at Ngaruawahia was abandoned before the troops arrived. Heavy fighting took place at Te Awamutu, and finally the warrior chief Rewi Maniapoto defied the Imperial soldiers at Orakau. It was here that one of the chiefs uttered the famous shout of defiance when the general in charge of the troops offered the defenders the opportunity of surrendering. "*E hoa, ka whawhai tonu ahau kia koe, ake, ake.*" (Friend, I will fight against you for ever,

A chief rejecting the request of General Cameron that the Maoris surrender at Orakau.

for ever.) The episode has been described as "the greatest
fight of forlorn hope in the history of the world—three
hundred men, women and children held at bay one thousand eight hundred British troops assisted by artillery and
cavalry".[1]

After three days the exhausted survivors were without
food and ammunition. They broke out of the *pa* and through
the ranks of soldiers in a desperate effort to escape. Many
of them were shot as they rushed from the stronghold.

The Waikato campaign ended at Orakau, but the fire in
the fern was then kindled on the east coast. Supplies of food
and ammunition had been sent from the Bay of Plenty, but
the loyal Arawas of Rotorua had prevented the east coast
tribes from coming to the aid of those in the Waikato. On
the collapse of the Kingite cause there, the conflict shifted
to the east coast and reached its zenith at Tauranga, where
the Maoris put up a gallant defence at the Gate Pa in April
1864. Knowing they would be unable to hold the *pa*, they
retreated to Te Ranga, where they met their final defeat.
This campaign was notable for the chivalry and humanity
of a number of the Maori warriors.

In Taranaki the war lingered on in a desultory fashion
and then flared up fiercely into a kind of perverted *jehad*.
Te Ua, a *tohunga* who had received a mission education,
introduced an element of Old Testament teaching into a
new religion of his own devising. He claimed to have received
a call from the Archangel Gabriel to save his people from
the usurpers who had stolen his people's land. If they
chanted the words *Hapa, hapa, paimarire hau*, as they went
into battle, no harm could come to them, he claimed. The
bullets would then have no effect. That the incantation
often failed to preserve his followers was obviously due to
lack of faith. The name Hauhau was given to the converts

to the Paimarire religion on account of their battle cry
Hou hau, which sounded like the barking of dogs.

Hauhauism spread rapidly from Taranaki to Waikato, to
the Bay of Plenty, to the East Coast, and to Hawke's Bay.
The Hauhaus were guilty of revolting practices. At Opotiki
a CMS missionary, the Rev C.S. Volkner, was murdered and
mutilated, and other atrocities committed. The consequences of this wave of pseudo-religious fanaticism that
united many of the tribes as effectively as the King Movement had done might well have proved disastrous to Maori
as well as Pakeha. But gradually the superior equipment of
the British troops, who were now supported by settlers ex-
perienced in bush warfare, and the assistance of their Maori
allies, overcame the fierce opposition of the Hauhaus.

One final act of defiance originated with the famous
warrior Te Kooti. It would seem that he was imprisoned
unjustly and sent with a number of Hauhaus to the Chatham
Islands. Three years of imprisonment turned him into a
dangerous, embittered man—one who shared with Te Ua a
belief that he had been divinely appointed to be the saviour
of his people. The warders of the prison camp were over-
powered, a schooner seized, and a horde of bloodthirsty
warriors commenced a reign of terror on the east coast,
murdering defenceless settlers. As resistance was organised
Te Kooti led his followers deep into the forested regions
of the Urewera, where they eluded pursuit for four years.
The Government offered a reward of £5000 for his capture
but in vain. Eventually he escaped to the area known as the
King Country—a region where no white man dared venture
after the fighting ceased.

*

It was not until 1881 that the Maori King laid his arms

at the feet of Major William Mair, who had often pursued Te Kooti.

"It is peace," said King Tawhiao. "There will be no more trouble."

The wars between Maori and Pakeha was officially ended, but the aftermath was bitterness and suspicion. Heavy losses had been sustained on both sides. The country was impoverished by the cost of the war, the rebels were dispirited, and much of their land confiscated.

References 1. *Tuwharetoa*, J. Te H. Grace. A.H. & A.W. Reed

CHAPTER 7

AFTERMATH OF WAR

He tao huata e taea te karo,
he tao na aitua e kore.

The thrust of a war spear may be parried,
but not the spear of misfortune.

THE LAST twenty years of the nineteenth century were
the most gloomy in Maori history. The *mana* of a proud
people had apparently been destroyed for ever. Defeat alone
was sufficient to bring despondency, but there were other
factors too. Nearly three million acres of their best land had
been confiscated to compensate the Government for the
cost of the war and to provide land for settlement. The
brief days of Maori prosperity were over. Faith in the
Pakeha religion was shaken, for it was suspected, unjustly,
that the missionaries had abandoned the Maori in the hour
of his greatest need. In 1865 the Government had set up a
system of Native Land Courts, with the best of intentions,
and had relinquished its pre-emptive right of purchase. In
practice this meant that Pakehas could now purchase land
direct from individual Maoris. Thus communal rights were
abrogated, and the *mana* of the *ariki* eroded. These and
other influences had probably encouraged the rapid spread
of Hauhauism, for in this religion the *tohunga* had reasserted
their power. Now that the war was over the opportunity for
individuals, no longer restrained by the power of the *ariki*,
to sell land, put them at the mercy of unscrupulous Pakehas,
who plied them with drink, cheated them of their rights,

Maori women preparing potatoes at the village of Parihaka, about 1900. (Alexander Turnbull Library)

and persuaded them to sell land for a fraction of its real value.

Added to these indignities was a decline in population, due to introduced diseases such as tuberculosis, pneumonia, and typhoid. The squalid, insanitary conditions in which many Maori communities were now forced to live increased their susceptibility to disease. It has been said that "there is no need to conjure up some mysterious psychological fatalism which was driving the people to extinction"[1]; but the loss of *mana* must not be forgotten as a contributing factor in the decline of the Maori population over a twenty-year period from 58,000 to about 40,000.

A group of Maoris in Parihaka pa in the 1880s. (Alexander Turnbull Library)

During this depressing period there were Pakehas who were deeply concerned at the fate of the Maori, but the most they could do, in terms of a currently popular phrase, was "to smooth the pillow of a dying race".

Writing of the phenomenon of Hauhauism in a penetrating assessment of Maori life, Erik Schwimmer remarked that "the despair of the 1860s and of succeeding years has left a mark that has by no means faded, even in the present day. Very few are now Hauhau, but the land wars, the confiscations, the disintegration of tribal life, the breaking of the *mana*, all of which are behind the despair of the Hauhau chants, these have for ever driven out the naive acceptance of the Pakeha of the 1840s and 1850s."[2]

Although the King Movement had succeeded in creating a loose confederation of tribes) though with a number of notable exceptions), and the King Country provided a refuge for dissidents for some years after the wars were over, it seemed impossible to envisage any hope of independent Maori existence. A propher and leader in Taranaki, Te Whiti, had attempted to organise passive resistance at Parihaka, but this too failed when a force of militia was despatched to quell the resistance movement.

"If the blood of our people only had been spilled," said Ngapora Tamati of Waikato, "then this trouble would have been over long ago."

References   1. *The Story of the Maori People.* G.L. Pearce. Collins.
            2. *The World of the Maori.* Erik Schwimmer. A.H. & A.W. Reed

CHAPTER 8

NEW HOPE

Ahakoa he iti te matakahi,
ka pakaru i a au te totara.

Although the wedge is small, by it the
totara tree will be shattered.

TO CHANGE the metaphor of the proverb in the heading of this chapter, there was one gleam of light in the darkness of the 1880s and 1890s. Maori parents had begun to realise that their race's hope of survival lay with their children and that, in order for them to gain a place in the Pakeha world, they needed to be educated. It was not a new idea. As we have seen, mission schools had catered for Maori education up to the time of the wars. As early as 1844 State schools had been provided for Maori children. In 1867 and again in 1871 Native Schools Acts made provision for their education. One of the clauses stipulated that instruction should be given in English, a decision that appeared logical if the children were to take their place in the world of Pakeha culture.

In a recent interview[1], D.G. Ball, who was appointed Senior Inspector of Maori Schools in 1937, stated that "Maori children were not even allowed to speak Maori in the playground. If they did they would probably be punished. The purpose was quick assimilation—forget your Maori side and get our side. This was the recognised philosophy of the western world. We knew nothing of anthropology, we knew nothing of the importance of a culture,

101

of the development of a personality. We imagined that you could drop a culture, pick up another one . . . Well, you just can't do that sort of thing; we know that now but we didn't know it then."

We do indeed know it now, but only after a long apprenticeship in understanding. Nevertheless there was a sincere attempt to provide for the education of Maori children. Although a disappointingly small number carried their education through to secondary level, intentions were good. Land for schools was frequently donated by the Maori community, and the older people encouraged the younger generation.

The most significant development in the field of education was the Maori Boys' college at Te Aute in Hawke's Bay. Under the leadership of a brilliant headmaster a group

Maori women in European dress about 1890. (Alexander Turnbull Library)

Te Aute College, Hawke's Bay, the famous Maori boys' school where many great leaders were educated. (Alexander Turnbull Library, Alexander Collection)

of students formed an association which, after several changes of name, became known as the Young Maori Party. The members included a number of gifted students—Apirana Ngata, Maui Pomare, Te Rangihiroa (Peter Buck), all of whom were later knighted after an outstanding career in the service of their people—and Reweti Kohere, Tutere Wirepa, and others. They were convinced they had a mission to restore pride of race to their people.

The first problem was to raise standards of health and housing as a prelude to a revival of *maoritanga*, a term that sums up all that is best in Maori culture.

In 1900 the Public Health and Maori Councils Act was passed which required the appointment of a Native Health Officer. The position was offered to Maui Pomare, who had an uphill battle in front of him. As a Maori speaking to his own people he wielded more influence than any Pakeha

Fourth-form students at the Queen Victoria School for Maori Girls, Auckland. (National Publicity Studios)

officer could have achieved. Gradually his work began to bear fruit.

By 1912 Pomare, Ngata, and Buck were all members of Parliament. To understand the background we must return to the 1880s. James Carroll, equally well known by his Maori name of Timi Kara, was a man of limited education but large ideas. As a young man he had taken part in the campaign against Te Kooti. In 1887 he entered Parliament which, since 1868, had included four Maori electorates, as it still (1973) does. After six years as the Member for Eastern Maori he contested the European seat of Waiapu (now Gisborne) successfully and retained it for twenty-six years.

Sir James Carroll, 1857-1926, Maori
Member of Parliament and one-time
Acting Prime Minister of New Zealand.
(Alexander Turnbull Library)

Sir Apirana Ngata, former Minister of
Maori Affairs. (Alexander Turnbull
Library, S.P. Andrew Collection)

A born orator and a powerful advocate for his people, Carroll was instrumental in introducing legislation that paved the way for later innovations by members of the Young Maori Party. During his Parliamentary career he became Minister for Native Affairs and for a time held the position of Acting Prime Minister. He was knighted in 1911. During his term of office the Native Land Act, by which Maori land could be sold only through Maori Land Councils, was passed. No longer could the wily Pakeha tempt a Maori to dispose of land for less than its worth.

The disastrous attrition of the post-war years was slowly and surely coming to an end. In 1926 a Royal Commission admitted the injustice of the Waitara purchase, the branding of men who were fighting for their rights as rebels, and the confiscation of land. The rightful owners of the Waitara purchase could no longer be identified, but compensation was made to the tribal owners, through the Taranaki Maori Trust Board, of an annual grant of $5000. The principle of compensation is still recognised, the yearly amount paid to ten Trust Boards now exceeding $300,000.

On his appointment to the office of Minister of Maori Affairs, Sir Apirana Ngata was active in encouraging the co-operative working and ownership of land by family groups. With the assistance of the Trust Boards large areas of useless land were brought into cultivation, and more than 2000 farms established. Ngata was also instrumental in reviving interest in the ancient arts—carving, weaving, songs, dances, and genealogical lore—without which there could be no hope of national revival.

As standards of living improved, the Maori population increased dramatically. The pillow of a dying race was thrown aside as a new consciousness of racial strength and independence was roused. The formation of a Maori Battalion in World War I, the appointment of a Bishop of Aotearoa to care for the Maori section of the Anglican Church, and the establishment of a number of autonomous organisations were an indication of the strength of the resurgent pride of race.

The basic achievements of Sir James Carroll and the Young Maori Party were amicable discussion and legislation; as a result, they established a national and territorial *mana* that did not and could not be overturned.

References   1. *Education* No.3, 1973. School Publications Branch, Dept. of Education.

CHAPTER 9

THE MAORI TODAY

He kai na tangata, he kai titongitongi;
He kai na tona ringa, tino kai, tino makona noa.

You can only nibble at another's food, but with food you have
cultivated yourself, you can satisfy your appetite.

THIS PROVERB about food has relevance to Maori life
today. For 200 years the Maori has been nibbling the food
of the Pakeha. There have been times when he has found it
more satisfying than his own diet, times when it has been
repugnant. Today he realises that although the food of the
western world is essential to his health, the food that sustained his ancestors is equally necessary for survival.

If "culture" is substituted for "food", the truth of the
proverb becomes apparent. The Maori of today lives in two
worlds. The *mana* of his people is rooted in the past. It is
part of his being. If he loses this, he loses everything, for
then he is swallowed up by a strange and alien world.
Fortunately he has been able to adapt himself in large
measure to the western way of life and to acquit himself
creditably, while retaining the life principle that contributed
to the ethos of the Maori race.

In considering the situation of the New Zealand Maori
in the 1970s a problem of definition arises. There are few
now who claim to be full-blooded Maoris. Intermarriage has
not diminished the Polynesian, but has added to his strength.
Sir Peter Buck (Te Rangihiroa) said of himself that he was
binominal, bilingual, and an inheritor of two bloods which

107

he would not have changed "for a total of either"—a statement that could well be applied to the majority of Maoris today.

The problem of definition, however, still remains. For census purposes all persons of half or more than half Maori ancestry are classed as Maoris. For Parliamentary elections persons of more than half Maori ancestry register in one of the four Maori electoral districts, while those of half Maori ancestry have the option of registering on either a Maori or European roll.

Maoritanga. From this it will be seen that the Maori has integrated with but has not been absorbed by the European community. The danger was there, long ago, but it has been avoided. One of the most encouraging features of the present time is the revival of interest in *maoritanga*, in some cases with pristine purity and fidelity, in others retaining its essential features but adapted to the twentieth century. Unless carried to extremes, these are healthy tendencies. There is still a place for the craftsman.

The huge *pouihi* (a kind of totem pole) carved by Inia te Wiata and erected in New Zealand House in London in 1972 is no less a tribute to the heritage of the past because it was sculpted by a modern craftsman with steel tools. Inia was a true *tohunga whakairo rakau* (expert in woodcarving). It is said that he meticulously observed the hallowed conventions that attend such work. Every chip, for instance, was disposed of reverently in the accepted manner. Similarly Inia bridged two cultures by his singing in the world's great opera houses.

The same can be said of the modern action song that has become a feature of Maori concerts. In essence it is a development of the *haka waiata* or posture dance. According to Alan Armstrong and Reupena Ngata[1] it is "a summing up

Sir Peter Buck chats with Sir Bernard Freyberg, Governor-General of New Zealand, after his investiture (1949). (National Publicity Studios)

Ikaroa Maori Group performing at Gisborne during the 1953 Royal visit. One in three performers is a Pakeha who has won a place in the group through ability. (National Publicity Studios)

of the whole of modern Maori culture. It typifies a harmonious blending of the old and the new, it embodies the music and the poetry which is the very soul of the race, and above all, it is a vigorous expression of the pride and of the hopes and aspirations for the future which are the great motivating force of the Maori people today."

Population. The growth rate of the Maori population is twice that of the total population. In itself this has some bearing on present-day problems and achievements. The nineteen-sixties and seventies have seen what has been described as the greatest Polynesian migration in history—the Maori movement from country into town. In 1936 only 8000 out of a total population of 80,000 Maoris lived in cities and boroughs. In 1970 there were over 125,000— more than half the Maori population. Another important factor in assessing the situation is that more than 60 per cent of Maoris are under the age of twenty-one, compared with 43 per cent of the population as a whole, 50 per cent under fifteen years of age compared with 33 per cent. The average Maori of adult years therefore has a greater number of dependants than the Pakeha, and, on the average, a lower income.

As the Ombudsman, Sir Guy Powles, pointed out in an address to the 20th Conference of the Maori Women's Welfare League in 1972, there is a danger in making comparisons on a proportional basis between the Maori population, the Pakeha population, and the total population, firstly because of the difficulty of defining "Maori" exactly, secondly because of the influx of other Polynesians from the Pacific Islands. He reminded his hearers that in law the Maori is a British subject and a New Zealand citizen, with all the rights and status the law confers. In addition there are legal provisions that apply to the Maori and the Maori alone. The latter include Parliamentary representation, finance, housing, land courts, education, wardens, and other matters dealt with in the Maori Welfare Act of 1962.

The Maori Community. Certain notable changes in location and living conditions during the past twenty or thirty years have tended at first to fragment, but latterly to contribute to, the feeling of racial identity. The days of the *whanau*, the large family group, and the *hapu*, the larger sub-tribe or extended family unit, are over. Rural areas of concentration have become scattered, but retain the com-

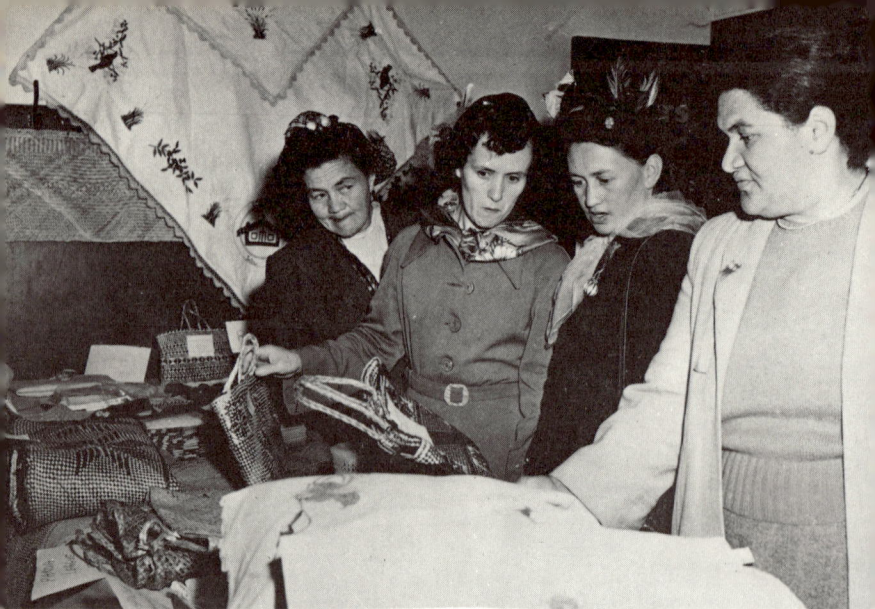

Maori Women's League Welfare workers examining a handicraft exhibition at their 1953 Conference. (Alexander Turnbull Library)

munity spirit. Farmers work together, foregather at funerals (*tangi*), feasts (*hui*), and public gatherings. Those who have left the tribal lands return for these celebrations, breaking down the barriers that have separated them from their kinsfolk.

In towns and cities families tend to cluster together, often in poorer areas and in substandard conditions, owing to the high cost of suburban housing, or in newly developed State housing groups. The denser housing in the cities provides opportunities for the preservation of the spirit of the *marae* in community centres, which is an important factor in maintaining the distinctive culture and "wholeness" of the Maori people; but admittedly there is not quite the same participation by the whole community as in the days of the *hapu* and *whanau*.

Modern Maori houses at Koutu, Rotorua County, built in the early 1950s. (Alexander Turnbull Library)

It is difficult for a Pakeha to enter into the life and feeling of a Maori community. Pressure, no matter how well intentioned, will be met with reserve. Erik Schwimmer has summed up the situation: "Every Maori learns from childhood certain distinctive attitudes which can be expressed in three structural attitudes. The Maori people is viewed as a socio-religious unity, the Maori local community as a basic unit of cooperation and an object of unswerving loyalty, the extended family or quasi-familial neighbourhood or work group as a primary source of emotional and economic support."[2]

Employment. Maoris are most at ease when working together as a team. Their standards are different from those of their European counterparts. Contrary to some popular belief they have a capacity for hard work, but not that of

113

Farm hand in the Te Aroha district. (National Publicity Studios)

the nine-to-five clock-watching Pakeha. There are times for work, times for relaxation and enjoyment, times for dropping everything to submerge themselves in the comfort of belonging to each other, of being one people.

Nevertheless Maori and Pakeha can and do work side by side in complete amity and in many occupations. These occupations are to a large extent unskilled, though one can find Maoris handling huge earth-moving equipment with nonchalent ease, driving buses and trucks with unobtrusive competence and good nature. It has been suggested that this is a stereotype, but there is no doubt that Maoris are frequently employed in such ways. Only too frequently opportunities for advancement are limited by low educational standards which often stem from a home environ-

Maori air hostess with National Airways Corporation.
(National Publicity Studios)

ment where the Maori language is the mother tongue. Much is being done to improve educational standards; much yet remains to be done. It must not be supposed that intellectual level is low: an increasing number of younger Maoris have entered the nursing, teaching, and other professions and, in teaching, are improving the educational standards of Maori children.

Language. Many young people are leaders in the search for a national identity. They want the food of their own culture, the food they have cultivated themselves, as well as the best the Pakeha can offer. One of the most debated issues of the day is whether there should be compulsory teaching of the Maori language not only to Maori pupils but also to interested Pakeha children. Of the 5700 young people learning Maori in secondary schools in 1972, more than a third were Pakehas. Mutual awareness and respect is an indication of a growing together of the two races, allied with pride in their separate origins.

Language has an important part to play. In *Te Maori*[3] , May 1973, Terry Ball Writes: "If Maori is to remain a living, vigorous language and an integral part of *maoritanga*, it must survive in the *marae* environment. But the cities are notoriously lacking in *marae*, so the language is in danger of gravitating toward that fusty academic world where Latin is still king." There is certainly an element of truth in this statement, but in the same article Dr Rangi Walker is quoted as saying, "It's terrific to see the number of young people who use Maori at every opportunity . . . There are enough people around who fight to keep the language alive, even in suburban surroundings."

Without the language, in which the culture is enshrined, all will be lost. *Toi te kupu, toi te mana, te whenua*—the permanence of the language, prestige, and land—these are the treasures that are now in the nation's hands.

Aspects of Discrimination. In spite of enthusiasm it must be admitted that there are problems amongst young people of Maori descent, and that the Maori has a higher crime rate than the national average. There are several causes—sudden transition from rural to suburban life, lower educational standards, and problems of accommodation. The Maori's difficulties in understanding legal subtleties and in expressing himself can also lead to a higher rate of conviction. As the Ombudsman has shown, the high proportion of young people has an effect on the statistics of crime, and the fact that "persons who are less than half Maori have been willing to classify themselves as Maoris in the courts, although they may not do so for census purposes".

Maori children at Orakei Play Centre. Mothers supervise all activities of these pre-school youngsters. (National Publicity Studios)

One other factor must also be recognised: popular opinion is influenced by newspaper reports in which a Maori is often identifiable by his name—a fact that tends to exaggerate racial identification. The channelling of energies into worthwhile activity is a challenge to all who are interested in the welfare of all youth, either Maori and Pakeha. The New Zealand Maori Council feels that because Maori children find little of relevance to their cultural ethos in school they tend to succeed in sport but fail in academic achievement. As the pupils opt out of school they swell the numbers of the "brown proletariat", or join the urban gang in search of their own identity.

George Nepia, the famous All Black, shaking hands with Frank Kilby before a match. (Alexander Turnbull Library)

The New Zealander of European origin is proud of the Maori people and accords them a degree of admiration that can be found in no other country where there is racial co-existence. The prospect of fielding a national Rugby football team that excludes Maoris would now be intolerable. It happened once but can never happen again. Yet problem areas still remain, particularly in housing, sometimes with apparent reason. The warmhearted hospitality and communal spirit of the Polynesian are calculated to burst the seams of conventional decorum, often to the annoyance of neighbours—but this is not necessarily solely a Maori trait:

there are Pakeha parties that are even more disturbing to tired neighbours robbed of sleep in the small hours.

The Race Relations Act passed in 1971 now makes any form of discrimination on racial grounds a punishable offence. It does not mention Maoris specifically. It is a stern reminder that in the modern world tolerance must be accorded to people of every nationality.

Religion. The work of Christian missionaries was largely destroyed by the wars of the nineteenth century. There followed a period of uncertainty, an eager grasping of millennial cults founded on Old Testament teaching intermingled with fragments of Maori primitive beliefs. Hauhau-

Ceremonial house (Turongo) of the Maori Queen, at Turangawaewae Pa, Ngaruawahia. (National Publicity Studios)

The Maori Queen, Dame Te Ata-i-Rangikaahu. (Evening Post)

ism had its day and declined. Ringatu, a relic of Te Kooti's messianic faith, still lingers on. The Catholic, Church of England, Methodist, Presbyterian and other churches have retained a number of adherents. In recent years Mormonism has gained many converts. Unlike the orthodox churches, the New Zealand Church of Latter-day Saints has no Maori section, but about 70 per cent of its New Zealand membership is Maori.

A distinctive Maori faith, in which millennial doctrine and faith-healing play an important part, along with traditional and Christian beliefs, and with its emphasis on the importance of genealogies, is that of the Ratana church. Several Maori prophets have claimed to have received a message from God. Tahupotiki Wiremu Ratana received such a message in 1920. "The only source of authority he recognised," wrote Schwimmer, "came from God and reached the Maori people through his mediation as *mangai* (mouth). His followers are known as the *morehu*, the remnant, which implies that they are the common people salvaged from the wreckage of a collapsed culture. Ratana offers not only a religious reorientation on a Christian basis, but also of political restoration based on what is seen as the realisation of the promise of the Treaty of Waitangi."

Ratana adherents number about 13 per cent of the Maori population. They exercise a considerable influence politically as well as in other ways, Ratana candidates have been prominent in politics for many years.

The Maori Queen. It is not possible in this brief account of Maori life to mention the many men and women who have achieved distinction in two worlds, but even a record as brief as this would be incomplete without mention of the Maori Queen. Her authority is not recognised by all tribes for, as we have seen, a number refused to join the King

Princess Te Puea Herangi, a prominent Maori leader who helped to revive maoritanga. *(National Publicity Studios)*

Miss Elizabeth Mountain, a Maori art student at Elam School of Fine Arts, Auckland. (National Publicity Studios)

Movement at its inception. But by her gracious personality Queen Ata-i-Rangikaahu, the first queen in Maori history, has again proved that women of noble ancestry and personal *mana* can heal longstanding breaches. Earlier in this century Princess Te Puea, to whose energy and devotion the building of the royal residence Turangawaewae at Ngaruawahia was due, won the respect of Maori and Pakeha. The influence of women is now clearly emphasised in the work on the Maori Women's Welfare League.

This in turn is symptomatic of Maori unity on a national scale. In earlier years tribal strengths and loyalties prevented their people from speaking with one voice, but national as well as regional identity is now being achieved on several fronts. The structure of a society within a society, concerned with the welfare of its own people yet part of the larger community, is growing apace.

Maori arts are flourishing. The work of artists, poets, composers, and sculptors of both sexes is evidence of the fact that there can be a fusion of cultures that still retains the distinctive contribution of their separate racial origins.

References   1. *Maori Action Songs.* Alan Armstrong and Reupena Ngata. A.H. & A.W. Reed
2. *The World of the Maori.* Erik Schwimmer. A.H. & A.W. Reed
3. *Te Maori.* May 1973. The New Zealand Maori Council.

CHAPTER 10

THE MAORI TOMORROW

*Tungia te ururua kia tupu
wahakaritorito te tupu o te harakeke.*

Set the overgrown bush alight, and the
new flax shoots will spring up.

THE REV KINGI IHAKA interprets this proverb as: Burn
or dispose of whatever hinders progress in all that is done,
in order that what is desirable may indeed grow and bear
fruit.

The key to tomorrow lies in the hands of the young
people of today. To quote yet another proverb from the
rich store of Maori lore: *Mate atu he tete kura, whakaeke
mai he tete kura*—a fern frond dies, another frond rises to
take its place.

The young people have accepted the challenge. The
tourist will enjoy the spirited performance of the *haka
waiata*, the stick games, the rhythm and movement of the
poi dance, the colourful costumes, but he will see little or
nothing of the movements that are creating a race of people
with newly-kindled pride in their ancestry, who are also
citizens of equal status with their Pakeha friends.

There have been farseeing Maoris who have foretold that
continued intermarriage will eventually result in a new race
with the blood of two noble races in their veins. In the
coming years it may well be so, but the time is not yet.
There are Pakehas who have made the same prophecy, but
with a different meaning: to them integration has meant

Hon. Mrs Whetu Tirikatene-Sullivan MP, first Maori woman to attain Cabinet rank in New Zealand. (National Publicity Studios)

The Hon. Matt Rata, Minister of Maori Affairs and Minister of Lands in Labour Cabinet 1972. (National Publicity Studios)

that eventually those of Maori descent should realise that it will be an honour to be absorbed by, and lose their identity in, the life of a supposedly superior race.

The accomplishments of the Maori of today remove any thought of such a calamitous happening, but it is widely acknowledged that a new approach is needed in the education of the young. The New Zealand Maori Council is emphatic that any policy of assimilation should be replaced by a multicultural system of education. Its recommendations include permission for mothers to speak Maori to their children in pre-school precincts and that the programme should include Maori singing and dancing, and myths and folktales, increased provision for the teaching of the Maori language in primary schools, an extension of the teaching of Maori culture, visits to *marae*, and the inclusion of current trends such as the King Movement, Maori Committees, Women's Welfare Leagues; in secondary schools compulsory study of Maori as a second language, the formation of culture clubs, a study of contemporary Maori society starting with the great leaders such as Ngata, Pomare, and Buck, the prophetic movements, Maori politics, and emerging economic trends such as Maori cooperatives, incorporations, and credit unions.

A balance of one culture with another has not yet been achieved. Each must contribute to the welfare of the other. There must be mutual receiving as well as giving. There are many things that hinder progress towards the ultimate fulfilment of the dream of a wholly united nation. Educational standards must be raised. The richness and *joie de vivre* of the Maori must be shared by the Pakeha—his care for the aged, his delight in sharing in work and pleasure, his indifference to personal gain and position. It is equally important that the Maori should appreciate the virtues of the Pakeha culture.

Ko koe ki tena, ko ahau ki
tenei kiwai o te kete.

You at that and I at this handle of the basket.

GUIDE TO PRONUNCIATION

Note: In the written language the long vowels may be indicated by a macron, eg *pāhi* (past), or by doubling the vowel eg *paahi*. Reeds' *Concise Maori Dictionary* indicates long vowels in the Maori-English section by means of the macron. Every vowel is sounded: eg *mere* has two syllables, not one; Petone has three syllables, not two.

Short *a*, as in *manu*, like *u* in nut.
Long *a*, as in *mānu*, like *a* in Chicago.
Short *i*, as in *pipi*, like *i* in pit.
Long *i*, as in *pīpī*, like *ee* in peep.
Short *e*, as in *peke*, like *e* in peck.
Long *e*, as in *pēke*, like *ai* in pair.
Short *o*, as in *koko*, like *or* in report.
Long *o*, as in *kōko*, like *or* in pore.
Short *u*, as in *putu*, like *u* in put.
Long *u*, as in *pūtu*, like *oo* in moon.

GLOSSARY

ao: cloud, day
Aotearoa: Maori name for
New Zealand
ara: path
Arawa, Te: one of the canoes
of the Fleet
ariki: chief
aria: material representation
of an *atua*
aroha: affection, love
aronui: inclination, desire
ata: shadow, form
atua: god
aute: paper mulberry
awa: river, valley
haere mai: welcome
haere ra: farewell
haka: dance
hapu: sub tribe
hau: wind, breath
Hauhau: fanatical rebel
Haumia-tiketike: god of
fernroot
Hawaiki: the Homeland
he: a, this
heitiki: neck ornament
hinau: berry-bearing tree
hine: girl, young woman
Hine-ahu-one: the first
created woman
Hine-raumati: the summer
girl

hue: gourd plant
huia: extinct bird
Hui-te-Rangiora: legendary
explorer
ika: fish
Io: the supreme god
iti: small
iwi: tribe, bone
kahawai: fish
kai: food, to eat
kainga: unfortified village,
home
kaka: bush parrot
karaka: berrybearing tree
kauri: forest tree
kia ora: good health
kino: bad
kiore: rat
kiwi: wingless nocturnal bird
ko: digging stick
kore: nothing, nothingness
kotahitanga: oneness, unity
kumara: sweet potato
Kupe: legendary discoverer
of New Zealand
kupenga: net
Kurahaupo: one of the canoes
of the Fleet
kuri: dog
makutu: witchcraft
mana: influence, force,
prestige

manaia: beaked figure in wood carvings

Manaia: early arrival in New Zealand

manga: tributary, branch, stream

mangai: mouth

manu: bird

manuka: tea-tree

Maori: indigenous Polynesian inhabitant of New Zealand

maoritanga: the whole culture of the Maori people

marae: the site of ceremonial and other occasions

Mata-atua: one of the canoes of the Fleet

matua: parent

Maui: a demigod

maunga: mountain

mere: stone or greenstone club

moa: large extinct bird

moana: sea

moari: giant stride

moki: fish

moko: facial tattoo

morehu: survivor, remnant

motu: island

nga: the (plural)

Ngahue: companion of Kupe

nui: large, many

Nuku: pursuer of Manaia

o: of, the place of

one: beach, land

pa: fortified village

pai: good

Paimarire: the Hauhau religion

Pakeha: white man, stranger

papa: flat, ground covered with vegetation

Papa-tu-a-nuku: Mother Earth

pataka: storehouse

patu: club, striking weapon

patupaiarehe: white-skinned fairy

peruperu: war dance

po: night

poi: ball on string used in dance

pounamu: greenstone

puke: hill

puna: spring

Ra, Te: sun god

Rakaihautu: giant who dug lakes in South Island

rakau: tree, timber

rangatira: person of noble birth

Rangi-nui-e-tu-nei: Sky Father

Ratana: founder of modern Ratana religious and political organisation

raupo: bulrush, reed

Ringatu: religious faith established by Te Kooti

roa: long, broad, high

Rongo: god of peace and cultivated food

roto: lake

taiaha: quarter-staff

tohunga: expert, priest

tohunga ahurewa: high-class priest

tohunga whaihanga: expert in house building

tohunga whakairo: expert in tattooing

tohunga whakairo rakau: expert in carving

Toi: early arrival at the Bay of Plenty

Tokomaru: one of the canoes of the Fleet

Tonganui: son of the sea god

totara: forest tree

tukutuku: woven lattice work

Tu-matauenga: god of war and mankind

utu: revenge, payment

wai: water

wai maori: fresh water

wai tai: salt water

waiata: song

waka: canoe

waka huia: treasure chest

waka taua: war party

wananga: knowledge

weka: ground bird

whai: cat's cradle

whanau: family

whanga: harbour, bay

whare: house

whare whakairo: carved meeting house

whariki: floor mat

whata: elevated storage platform

Whatonga: grandson of Toi

whenua: land

Tainui: one of the canoes of the Fleet

Tane: forest god, god of nature

Tane-rore: personification of heated air of summer

Tangaroa: god of the sea

tangata: man

tangata whenua: original inhabitants

tangi: funeral and funeral ceremony

taniwha: monster

tapu: sacred, forbidden

tarakihi: fish

taro: root vegetable

taua: war party

taumanu: resting place

Tawhaki: god of thunder and lightning

Tawhiri-matea: god of winds

te: the (singular)

tena koe: greetings (to one person)

tena korua: greetings (to two persons)

tena koutou: greetings (to several people)

toetoe: pampas grass

INDEX

134

135

FOR FURTHER READING

MAORI LEGENDS *by A.W. Reed, illustrated by Roger Hart*
The reader is taken behind the scenes of Maori belief in the supernatural, to a world of gods, demigods, giants, fairyfolk and monsters. Imaginatively illustrated.

AN ILLUSTRATED ENCYCLOPEDIA OF MAORI LIFE
by A.W. Reed
A one-volume encyclopedia of information on all aspects of Maori life, art and customs, arranged alphabetically with copious cross references.
Illustrated on every page.

MYTHS AND LEGENDS OF MAORILAND *by A.W. Reed*
Maori legends presented in a lively fashion. On its first publication this book was awarded the Easter Glen medal for the best children's book published in New Zealand that year.
48 full-page illustrations.